GARLAND STUDIES ON THE ELDERLY IN AMERICA

edited by

STUART BRUCHEY
UNIVERSITY OF MAINE

A GARLAND SERIES

THE HOUSING DECISIONS OF ELDERLY HOMEOWNERS

PETER G. VANDERHART

GARLAND PUBLISHING, Inc.
NEW YORK & LONDON / 1995

Library of Congress Cataloging-in-Publication Data

VanderHart, Peter G. , 1963–
    The housing decisions of elderly homeowners / Peter G. VanderHart.
       p.   cm. — (Garland studies on the elderly in America)
    Includes bibliographical references and index.
    ISBN 0–8153–1890–1 (alk. paper)
    1. Housing—United States—Decision making.   2. Aged—Housing—
United States.   I. Title.   II. Series.
    HD7293.V36   1995
    363.5'946'0973—dc20   94–33822
                                                                        CIP

Printed on acid-free, 250-year-life paper
Manufactured in the United States of America

To Kristi and Ryan

CONTENTS

INTRODUCTION

For many households, decisions regarding housing are among the most dramatic they make. A home is usually both the household's largest consumer durable and the largest portion of its investment portfolio. A certain degree of status comes with home ownership, and moving from one's home may involve considerable disruption.

These factors are often more significant for the elderly than for others. A home may represent much more than a source of consumption services to them. It is often their only significant asset, and in many cases represents a lifetime of savings. It also provides a feeling of independence and may be a source of many memories. Older persons also tend to adapt less well to change, especially with respect to living conditions. Decisions regarding owner-occupied housing are therefore of tremendous importance to the elderly.

Not only are the elderly's home ownership choices important to the elderly themselves, they are also important to public policy makers and business. Several government programs have an impact on, or are affected by the elderly's choice of living arrangement. Some of these seem designed to help the elderly stay in their homes (such as heating subsidies and property tax deduction and deferment programs, or the fact that home equity is not usually included as an asset for welfare program qualification purposes), while others seem to encourage movement out of owner-occupied housing (subsidized rents in retirement communities and differential treatment of institutional versus in-home medical care).

The private sector also is linked with the elderly's home ownership decisions. Nursing home and in-home care services have become large industries, and volunteer organizations provide delivered meals and some maintenance services. Financial institutions are also affected, as evidenced by the recent popularity of home equity loans and the recent creation of private reverse mortgage programs.

Despite the importance of understanding these decisions to both public and private concerns, it appears that the process is not completely understood. To date research has not been able to clearly identify what considerations are most important to the elderly when making housing decisions. Specifically, research has been unable to tell us whether financial or demographic factors are the most important determinants of the housing decisions that the elderly make. This book seeks to shed some light on the topic. Although several kinds of housing changes are investigated, the work is particularly interested in examining housing changes that reveal something about the factors that cause homeowners to desire to dissave out of home equity, and the extent to which such moves are taken.

The book will attempt to explain the decision making behavior of the elderly with regards to housing by (1) examining previous work in the area and discussing the decision making process by which the elderly determine if they should make a housing change; (2) presenting a model representing this decision; and (3) presenting statistical work describing this phenomenon.

The structure of the work follows this plan: Chapter 1 reviews previous work in the area. Chapter 2 presents a mathematical model of the decision, and describes some tractable comparative statics. Chapter 3 describes the data used in the dissertation and presents some initial empirical results. Chapter 4 examines pooled cross-sectional limited-dependent variable analyses. Chapter 5 utilizes a dynamic programing technique in an attempt to uncover elderly households' underlying preferences regarding housing. Chapter 6 summarizes the results and discusses policy implications.

The results of this study indicate that the elderly may desire to use their accumulated home equity to finance consumption. It further shows that while financial factors play some role in the housing decisions of homeowners, demographic characteristics are much more important. The results therefore suggest that current housing policies designed to help older homeowners financially may indeed make them better off, but may have a limited effect on their decision to remain in their current home. Furthermore, because demographic characteristics are found to play such a strong role, policies that address the non-financial aspects of home ownership may be much more effective in allowing the elderly to remain in their homes.

ACKNOWLEDGMENTS

This work would not have been possible without the help of many people. I would like to thank Robert Haveman for his prompt and insightful comments that provided an excellent perspective on this work. I would also like to thank John Rust for his help with the dynamic programing analysis. Without his method and programing as an example, chapter 5 would not have been possible. I would especially like to thank Martin David for his patience and guidance from this work's very beginning until its completion.

The publication of this collection of research would not be possible had not several academic journals allowed me to include material that they had published earlier. Specifically, chapters 2 and 3 appear almost verbatim in two separate articles in *Journal of Housing for the Elderly* (Volume 11, No. 2, Reprinted by permission of The Haworth Press, Inc.). In addition, the first portion of chapter 4 appears in *Research on Aging* (Peter G. VanderHart, "A Binomial Probit Analysis of the Home Equity Decisions of Elderly Homeowners", RESEARCH ON AGING, Volume 15, No. 3, September 1993, pages 299-323, (c) Sage Publications, Inc., Reprinted by permission of Sage Publications, Inc.). The latter part of chapter 4 appears in *Journal of the American Real Estate and Urban Economics Association* (Peter G. VanderHart, "An Empirical Analysis of the Housing Decisions of Older Homeowners", JOURNAL OF THE AMERICAN REAL ESTATE AND URBAN ECONOMICS ASSOCIATION, Volume 22, No. 2, Summer 1994, pages 205-233, (c) 1994 The American Real Estate and Urban Economics Association, Reprinted by permission of The American Real Estate and Urban Economics Association). Portions of chapter 1 appear throughout these articles.

My Mother and Father provided me with much emotional support over the last years. Their interest and encouragement is much appreciated. I would also like to thank my wife, Kristi. Her support and understanding during the past years have been remarkable. The success of this research is made sweeter by sharing it with her.

The Housing Decisions
of Elderly
Homeowners

I. A REVIEW OF THE LITERATURE

HOUSING CHOICES OF ELDERLY HOMEOWNERS

In this first section the major types of housing changes undertaken by elderly homeowners are discussed. Evidence of the elderly's mobility is presented, and of those that move, the tenure choices they make is also presented. Although the evidence is rudimentary, it provides some information on the elderly's attitudes toward home ownership and home equity reduction.

Potential Housing Changes

The life-cycle and permanent income hypotheses concerning consumption imply that in later life households will draw down their assets to finance consumption. Given that owner-occupied housing often makes up such a large portion of the elderly's assets, it is not unreasonable to think that they may wish to reduce the amount of this asset in some way to increase consumption.

One way to enable dissaving out of home equity would be for the household to acquire a reverse mortgage. This instrument provides a flow of income without subjecting the household to moving costs. However, Manchester (1987) and Venti and Wise (1991) have observed that households with low incomes also tend to have low home equity, so low that a reverse mortgage would not provide substantial additional income to people who need it the most. In addition, the market for reverse mortgages was practically non-existent until a short time ago. Only about 100 had been written by 1984 (Weinrobe, 1984), and only in the last few years have private financial companies begun to offer reverse mortgages on a nationwide basis.[1]

If a reverse mortgage is unavailable or not desirable, some households may want to acquire a conventional mortgage or home equity loan to utilize their accumulated home equity. This action may be ill-suited for many elderly households because of the initial cost of any mortgage[2] and the interest rate difference between a mortgage and the investment of its proceeds. (See Appendix A of this chapter for an illustration.) Of course the acquisition of a mortgage does not necessarily entail a decrease in home equity: If the proceeds are used to remodel or improve the home, the equity of the home could increase. Also, although acquiring a mortgage may initially be an act of dissaving, it forces the household to save as the mortgage payments are made.

If an elderly household decides that acquiring a reverse or conventional mortgage is not a desirable alternative, it may decide to move to a home with lower equity or move into a rental unit. These sorts of moves would also allow the household to utilize its home equity to increase consumption. Although they would subject the household to the financial and psychic costs of moving, actions such as these could also allow the elderly to cut their housing expenditures, and the potentially smaller size of the new unit could be easier to maintain.

The homeowner may also find for various reasons that movement into a dependent living arrangement is optimal. These arrangements include living with children or with others, entering a nursing home or assisted-living community, or having one's housing paid for by others. These sorts of moves may also allow the household to increase consumption by drawing down home equity, but it is unclear whether the dependent elderly are able to enjoy the extra consumption.

Of course some homeowners may not want to reduce their home equity and may actually wish to increase it. As will be shown in later chapters, some of the elderly increase their home equity when they move. These sorts of moves are not necessarily at odds with life-cycle and permanent income models: Households may dissave only out of other assets, or a home may play a special role as a bequest.

All of the actions that tend to reduce home equity are consistent with life-cycle behavior in which the household holds a "lumpy" asset. It is this behavior (along with mortgage acquisition and moves that increase home equity) that will be described in the mathematical model of Chapter 2.

Mobility of the Elderly

One could point to the elderly's low rate of residential mobility as evidence that they are unlikely to dissave out of home equity by moving. Venti and Wise (1989) find that only about 27% of homeowners are observed to move during the 10 years of the Retirement History Survey (RHS), or about 3.1% per year. Feinstein and McFadden (1987) find slightly higher rates of residential change, approximately 4.5% per year, among aged homeowners in the Panel Study of Income Dynamics (PSID). For comparison, mobility rates of the non-elderly in the PSID are over 3 times that of elderly households (Reschovsky, 1990). Much higher rates, about 20%, are observed for households of all ages in Census of Housing data (Rosenthal, 1986).

Of course a low rate of residential change does not necessarily mean that the elderly do not wish to dissave out of home equity: Monetary and psychic moving costs may outweigh the benefits of the extra consumption provided, and some homeowners may find ways to tap home equity without moving.

Tenure Choice of the Mobile Elderly

The tenure choices of older households that move provide some evidence that the elderly wish to dissave out of home equity. James Poterba (in his comment on Venti and Wise, (1989)) presents transition probabilities for RHS respondents age 58 to 73 who moved during the 10-year survey period (1969-1979):

		New Tenure	
		Own	Rent
Previous	Own	.78	.22
Tenure	Rent	.17	.83

Little net movement out of home ownership is apparent in the previous matrix. However, Poterba also presents an analogous matrix from the 1973 Annual Housing Survey (AHS) for households older than 65:

		New Tenure	
		Own	Rent
Previous	Own	.61	.39
Tenure	Rent	.15	.85

Even though the information necessary for a rigorous statistical test is not included with these matrices, casual observation of the second matrix suggests significantly higher movement out of home ownership by the elderly. The difference between the two may be due to attrition bias in the RHS, or to the much younger age of those in the RHS: The AHS data include people of all ages over 65, and may reflect the retirement and health related moves of older households.

Feinstein and McFadden (1987) find similar results using data on persons over 65 from the PSID. They report the following matrix which includes an "other" category for those that live with their relatives or in a place of business:

		New Tenure		
		Own	Rent	Other
Previous	Own	.63	.26	.11
Tenure	Rent	.14	.81	.05
	Other	.26	.44	.30

In chapter 3 this matrix will be estimated for different age groups. The estimates reveal an increase in the proportion of moving owners that exit ownership as age increases past 65.

While rates of residential change and transition matrices contain some information about the elderly's housing decisions, they tell us little about changes in the amount of housing held or why such changes are made. Konrad Stahl

(1989) examines the former question using the PSID and a similar data set from Germany. He finds that aged households who move generally occupy less housing (measured by rooms per person) than those that don't. While Stahl's evidence suggests that the elderly reduce home equity, it may be deceiving for two reasons: (1) Housing changes that reduce the number of rooms do not necessarily reduce the level of home equity held; and (2) It is unclear whether movers actually reduce their housing or that movers merely tend to hold less housing (both before and after a move) than those who don't move.

In other work, Venti and Wise (1990) determine that older households that move from one owner-occupied unit to another are just as likely to increase home equity as to decrease it. Their analysis implies that if everyone in their sample were to move, the average home equity position would increase slightly. Venti and Wise conclude that the elderly have little desire to hold a lower level of home equity. However, they exclude from their sample those aged who completely liquidate their home equity by moving to a rental unit. The sample therefore ignores households who reduce home equity completely, and may tend to exclude owners of small homes whose only meaningful equity reduction is a complete liquidation.

Dependent Living Arrangements

As Feinstein and McFadden's matrix of the last section suggests, some households choose to switch into dependent living arrangements such as living with relatives, living in a nursing home, or having one's housing paid for by others. Using data from the PSID, Boersch-Supan (1989) finds that about one third of the elderly live in a dependent situation sometime before their death. He also finds that 14.4% share housing with relatives or friends at least for some time, and that 3.1% spend some time in an institution.

Kotlikoff and Morris (1988) report that since World War II, the elderly have increasingly tended to live alone (independently or in an institution), rather than with their children. They note that "Since 1940 the proportion of unmarried noninstitutionalized elderly living alone has risen from less than 25% to over 60%." Over the same period, the percentage of those elderly over 85 living in institutions has risen from 7% to nearly 25%. This may be in part due to the preferences of their children, who may rather pay for retirement housing or institutionalization than care personally for their parents.

These studies suggest that movements into dependent living arrangements are a fairly common housing alternative for homeowners. They also suggest that they are becoming increasingly popular and that they should be included in any analysis of housing decisions of older homeowners.

Mortgage Acquisition

Despite the disadvantages described in Appendix A, the available evidence indicates that a significant number of the elderly acquire new mortgages. In the 1987 American Housing Survey (AHS) (1989), over 20% of the elderly with mortgages (about 3.5% overall) reported that they acquired their current mortgage after they purchased their home. (See chapter 3 for additional evidence.) However there does not appear to be much desire by the elderly to acquire multiple mortgages: Results from Hobbs, Keest, and DeWaal (1989), (using Federal Reserve Board data), and Manchester and Poterba (1989), (using Survey of Income and Program Partici-pation data) show that less than 2% of homeowners age 65 and over hold multiple mortgages.

FACTORS AFFECTING THE CHOICE

In this section the factors frequently mentioned as the major determinants of elderly homeowners' housing decisions are discussed. After each discussion the results of past empirical studies are presented to show the extent to which the factor plays a role in the housing decision. The section begins with financial factors, and moves on to demographic and psychological considerations.

There is little previous evidence regarding the deter-minants of mortgage behavior and it is not discussed here. Also, recent literature concerned with moves into dependent living arrangements has dealt with all transitions from independent to dependent arrangements and has not isolated these kinds of changes that originate with home ownership. Thus, evidence presented for transitions to dependency also include renters and tend not to examine housing character-istics as causal factors.

Home Equity

Many studies have observed that elderly households tend to hold a large portion of their (non-social security) wealth in the form of owner-occupied housing. Using data from the RHS, Merrill (1984) reports that over two thirds of the elderly own their home. She observes that on average home equity makes up over 70% of the elderly's total wealth portfolio. Moreover, the AHS (1989) reports that 83% of elderly homeowners have no mortgage debt attached to their home equity. Similar results are found by Ai, Feinstein, McFadden, and Pollakowski (1990). Using the PSID they observe home equity to make up over half of the net worth of those in their sample over age 65. Similarly, Venti and Wise (1989) find that median home equity and financial assets are approximately equal when using a slightly different sub-sample of the RHS.

Like any other asset, home equity might be held as a bequest, for precautionary purposes, or to finance consump-tion in the future. As an asset, owner-occupied housing has the somewhat unique characteristic of providing services while one holds it. This adds a wrinkle to a household's decision that is not present with ordinary assets: The household must balance the value of the home as a consumer durable against the value of the consumption it could provide. As a homeowner becomes older, the value of the home appreciates while health and family conditions will likely make home ownership less attractive compared to other living arrangements. Presumably at some time the value of extra consumption that could be provided by reducing home equity might surpass the value of the home as a consumer durable. At this point the homeowner may choose to reduce home equity in some manner. Intuitively, the greater the amount of home equity the household has, (everything else equal), the greater the potential benefit from its reduction.

This discussion suggests that home equity deserves special treatment in a model of home ownership decisions by the elderly. While many studies treat it the same as ordinary financial wealth, its unique characteristics make a separate treatment desirable.

The results of some previous studies appear to be at odds with the discussion presented above. Venti and Wise (1989), using RHS data find that homeowners with the lowest home equity (grouped by home equity quartile) are the most likely to move. They also find that homeowners with high home equity do not move at a rate much greater than average. Both observations seem to contradict the intuition of the previous discussion, where it is suggested that high levels of home equity should encourage moves that enable equity reduction. However, simple mobility rates by equity quartile may be misleading: It may be that moves by those with differing levels of home equity are systematically different from one another, and a univariate treatment does not control for other important factors that may be highly correlated with home equity.

Reschovsky (1990), using data from the PSID, estimates elderly homeowners' potential benefits from changing tenure and from moving to another owner-occupied home. He then reports characteristics of persons with various levels of benefit: Homeowners with high potential benefits from moving to another home tend to have higher levels of home value than average. However, he finds a small negative relationship between housing value and the potential gains from moving to a rental unit. Although the analysis uses home value rather than home equity, the results suggest that homeowners may gain from moving to owner-occupied homes that have less equity.

Using data from the RHS, Merrill (1984) performs multivariate logistic analyses on home equity's effect on the probability of various housing changes between 1969 and 1977. She finds that the household's amount of home equity appears to have a negative effect both on the probability that a homeowner moves to a different home, and on the probability that the homeowner becomes a renter. Merrill's results contradict the discussion above, but may be misleading for two reasons: 1) Homeowners that move into homes having greater equity confounds the interpretation of results for those moving to another home. 2) Since Merrill only selects those elderly that own or rent in both 1969 *and* 1977, she omits those that have died, moved into dependent living arrangements or have been lost in the intervening years. Since all of these changes are associated with housing change, the selectivity of her sample may be a problem.

There is little evidence on the effect of home equity on a household's propensity to move into dependent living arrangements. Garber and Macurdy (1989), using National Long-Term Care Demonstration data find that home ownership tends to reduce a household's propensity to enter a nursing home. However no evidence is provided indicating the effect of the level of home equity on nursing home entrance.

Financial Assets

Intuitively, households with greater amounts of non-housing assets are less prone to dissave by reducing home equity. Wealthier households are better able to dissave out of their liquid assets to enhance consumption or pay for an unexpected expense. This allows them to avoid the transaction costs associated with reducing home equity, while they still enjoy the benefits that home ownership provides.

Note that these discussions imply that financial assets will deter moves that reduce home equity, while the amount of home equity held will promote such moves. Any rigorous treatment will therefore recognize that both home equity and financial assets are important in the explanation of the elderly's housing decisions, and that each should receive their own separate role in any analysis.

Past empirical studies provide mixed evidence on the effect of financial assets on homeowners mobility and tenure choice decisions. Venti and Wise (1989) find very little difference in mobility rates when they separate homeowners into financial asset quartiles. In other work (Venti and Wise, 1990), they find a negative relationship between wealth and desired housing equity. The former study may be misleading for two reasons: They exclude those homeowners that move into rental units, and they define "wealth" as financial assets *plus* home equity, while the discussion presented above suggests that financial assets and home equity have opposite effects on a homeowner's home equity decision.

Feinstein and McFadden (1987) use data from the PSID and a similar definition of wealth and find mixed results for wealth's effect on the mobility of homeowners. They find a weak positive relationship between the change in home equity of those that move and their measure of wealth. As with the results of Venti and Wise, these results may be inaccurate because they use a measure of wealth that includes both financial assets and home equity.

Further mixed evidence is found by Merrill (1984). She finds that liquid assets (bank accounts, stocks, and bonds) significantly increase the probability that a homeowner becomes a renter, but that illiquid assets (equity in professional practices and real estate) have an opposite effect. Both measures of assets had small and statistically insignificant effects on the probability that a homeowner purchases another owner-occupied home.

Little work has been done on the effect of assets on movement to dependent living arrangements.

Income

Income is expected to have an effect similar to that for financial assets: The more income a household has, the less its need to dissave out of any asset (including home equity) to finance consumption or pay for unexpected expenses. As is the case with home equity and financial assets, an appropriate model of the home ownership decisions of the elderly is not complete without the inclusion of income.

A large number of articles report on the effect of income on the housing changes of the elderly. Venti and Wise (1989) present evidence showing that RHS homeowners in the highest and lowest income quartiles are more likely to move than those closer to the median. Feinstein and McFadden (1987), using probit analyses on elderly homeowners in the PSID find that income has a positive but statistically insignificant effect on mobility. However, when they include dummy variables to indicate retirement status, the coefficient on income becomes negative. Reschovsky (1990) finds little relationship between a homeowner's income and potential benefit from moving to another owner-occupied home.

Feinstein and McFadden (1987) and Merrill (1984) both find that higher levels of income tend to cause moving homeowners to remain in the same tenure, although the effect in both studies is not statistically significant. Similarly, Reschovsky (1990) notes that homeowners with the least to gain from changing tenure tend to have higher levels of income. Merrill (1984) concurs, finding that income has a relatively strong inhibiting effect on the propensity of older homeowners to become renters.

Among homeowners that remain owner-occupiers upon moving, income appears to have a positive impact on the desired level of home equity. Venti and Wise (1989) find that owners in the highest income quartile who move consistently increase their home equity more (or decrease it less) than those in lower income quartiles. In other work (Venti and Wise, 1990), they use more sophisticated techniques and find that income has a statistically significant positive effect on the optimal level of home equity among elderly households.

There are many articles that deal with income's effect on elderly's moves to dependent living arrangements, but they do not draw a distinction between changes in which the household was previously owning and those in which they were renting. Nonetheless, since a large majority of the elderly are owners, it may be instructive to review the results of the following papers.

Several articles find that income has a negative effect on the propensity of the elderly to enter institutions. Boersch-Supan, Kotlikoff, and Morris (1988) utilize cross-sectional analyses on data from the Hebrew Rehabilitation Center for the Aged (HRCA) and find income to have a statistically significant negative effect on the incidence of becoming institutionalized. Using the same data and more rigorous econometric techniques Boersch-Supan, Hajivassiliou, Kotlikoff, and Morris (1990) concur. Boersch-Supan (1989) obtains very similar results using data from the PSID. Work by Ellwood and Kane (1989) and Garber and Macurdy (1989) using other data arrives at the same findings.

Income may also have an effect on the propensity of the elderly to live dependently with their children, other relatives, or friends. Boersch-Supan (1989) finds a negative relationship, although it is not statistically significant. Ellwood and Kane (1989) find a positive relationship, although it is not very strong. Kotlikoff and Morris (1988) find a negative relationship between the parent's income and the probability that they live with their children, and they note that the effect of children's income is even stronger.

The Out-Of-Pocket Cost of Housing

As mentioned above, many elderly households own their home outright, and thus have no mortgage payment. Still others are close to paying off the mortgage, and are thus likely to have relatively small payments to make on a favorable mortgage written long ago. Yet they must still make property tax payments, and provide for their home's maintenance. This may be difficult if the household is on a fixed income and the home's assessed value is large, maintenance costs are large or frequent, or the owners are unable to perform routine maintenance themselves. Of course high home ownership costs will only drive homeowners out of their house if a cheaper alternative is available. This suggests that both home ownership costs *and* the cost of alternative arrangements should be included in the discussion of elderly home ownership decisions.

There is some evidence to suggest that high costs of home ownership is a significant contributor to housing dissatisfaction among elderly homeowners. O'Bryant and Wolf (1983), using subjective responses from 464 homeowners over 60, found that on average elderly homeowners agreed with statements such as "My residence is costing me more than it's worth", and "My residence is a financial burden on me".

The alternative to paying the out-of-pocket costs of home ownership is a rental payment or other fee for alternative housing. To get the same flow of housing services from an alternative living arrangement, the household would likely pay a much larger sum than what they pay when owning. According to the 1987 AHS, the average monthly out-of-pocket housing cost for elderly homeowners is $213, while for elderly renters it is $306. This difference occurs despite the fact that the average number of rooms for elderly owners and renters is 5.5 and 3.7 respectively.[3] The size of this difference may be one of the factors leading to a household's desire to remain in a home, even when they consider home ownership a financial burden.

Only a few papers have directly examined the effect of housing costs on the decisions of elderly homeowners, and their results are contrary to the discussion above. Venti and Wise (1989) examine the change in out-of-pocket cost of housing of those homeowners in their sample who moved. They find that housing costs usually *increase* for those that move into rental units, and does not change much for those that move into other owner-occupied housing. This is inconsistent with the hypothesis that elderly homeowners may leave their homes to avoid out-of-pocket owning costs. Ai, Feinstein, McFadden, and Pollakowski (1990) include transactions costs and capital gains considerations in their imputation of a user cost of housing. Their results indicate that high user costs actually cause moving owners to remain owners and to buy larger homes. They explain this apparently counter-intuitive result by suggesting that the costs are higher in rapidly appreciating real estate markets where home owner-ship is a very attractive investment. Rosenthal (1986), using a sample of moving households of all ages in the PSID, finds that the relative user cost of owning to renting has a strong negative relationship with the probability that a moving household chooses to own.

Housing Characteristics

In addition to its equity value and cost, the charac-teristics of a home may also help determine the housing decisions of elderly homeowners. The floor area, number of rooms, and quality of structure may be valued by the homeowner. Because these factors are likely to be closely related to home equity and out-of-pocket cost, their inclu-sion in the analysis is necessary to avoid finding spurious relationships.

There is some disagreement as to whether the physical size of a home is an advantage or disadvantage for the elderly. Some authors have suggested that a large percentage of the elderly live in housing of "excess" size. (McFadden and Feinstein (1987), Lane and Feins (1985)). These authors suggest that some of the elderly may not be able to maintain their homes adequately, and may resort to closing off rooms or allowing maintenance problems to go unattended. However, Béland (1984), using data on elderly from Quebec, finds that living space per person is positively correlated with the elderly's desire to remain in their home. Reschovsky (1990) finds little relationship between potential gain from moving to a different home and number of rooms, and a small and counterintuitively negative relationship between number of rooms and benefit from becoming a renter.

Other authors have found evidence that housing quality can lead to attachment to a dwelling. Lawton (1980), using AHS data on elderly households finds that the age of structure, the presence of central heat, the number of bathrooms, and a number of other measures of housing quality are highly correlated with housing satisfaction.

The Home's Psychological Value

While a home is prized both for its monetary value and for the services it provides, older people may also value the home for separate psychological reasons. To the extent that these factors contribute to the attachment to a current home, they may also tend to effect a household's propensity to reduce home equity by moving. Given that in some cases the psychological attachment to a home may be strong, this is a factor that should not be ignored.

Gerontological studies indicate that the attachment to the home may be substantial. In a study of 320 homeowners over age 60, O'Bryant (1982) finds that subjective attitudes concerning home ownership explain more of the variance in housing satisfaction than do demographic of housing characteristics.[4] The measures of these attitudes include (1) competence in a familiar environment; (2) family orientation and memories; and (3) the status gained from home ownership itself. She also suggests that the length of residence in the home may increase the attachment to it. The implications of her work are further strengthened by Lawton (1980), who uses multivariate regression to find a strong correlation between home ownership and housing satisfaction.

Little has been done in the economics literature regarding the elderly's psychological attachment to the home. Reschovsky (1990) attempts to delve into this topic by estimating the potential gains that the elderly could achieve by moving. He concludes that there is substantial attachment to the home and suggests that this is a primary reason that elderly homeowners tend to "overconsume housing services". He does not observe a strong relationship between the length of residence in the home and the potential benefits from moving to another owner-occupied home or switching tenure.

Physical Limitations

Physical limitations and bad health may have an adverse effect on a homeowner's ability to maintain a house. A limitation can make some maintenance activities difficult, and could cause the elderly to have maintenance done by more expensive outside help. Limitations may also affect the homeowner's ability to perform everyday tasks in an independent living situation, thus causing a move to a dependent arrangement. If a physically limited or ill elderly homeowner has no children nearby and is financially constrained, one would expect them to be more prone to leave their home for an assisted-living arrangement. These considerations imply that inclusion of health and physical limitation in the analysis of the elderly's housing decisions is very important.

The literature generally shows no strong relationship between health factors and elderly households' propensity to reduce home equity. Venti and Wise (1989) find that an improvement in health reduces a homeowners propensity to move, and that a decrease in health has close to no effect. Merrill (1984) finds only a small statistically insignificant relationship between good health and the probability that a homeowner becomes a renter.

Several articles examine the effect of health on a household's propensity to enter an institution. Not surprisingly, most of these agree that bad and deteriorating health tends to precipitate moves into institutions. (See Garber and MaCurdy (1989), and Ellwood and Kane (1989).) Other work shows only a weak relationship between health and institutionalization when the measure of health is subjective, but a strong relationship when health variables are created from measures of functional abilities. (See Boersch-Supan, Kotlikoff, and Morris (1988).)

There is mixed evidence on health's effect on an older household's propensity to live with others. Boersch-Supan (1989) finds that health limitations are negatively associated with the elderly's odds of living dependently with others. However Kotlikoff and Morris (1989) find that the elderly who are comparatively more healthy are actually less likely to live with their children.

Familial Considerations

The presence of a spouse or children may also increase the attachment that a household has for a home. Each of the family members will experience disruption if a housing change is made, and a large household size is likely to find home maintenance easier and moving to a smaller home more inconvenient.

Even if the elderly's children do not live with them, their presence in the area may cause their parents to hold on to a home longer than otherwise. Independent children may be able to aid in the maintenance of the home, or care for the elderly in the home during short illnesses. Danziger, Schwartz, and Smolensky (1984) have suggested that elderly parents may hold homes of excess size as a form of insurance for their children, to be used as a refuge during spells of financial difficulty. The elderly's home may also be viewed as the center of an extended family, where they can meet for holidays and special occasions.

This discussion suggests that marital status, the number of children in the household, and the presence of independent children in the area all may play a role in the elderly's home ownership decisions.

There are a significant number of articles that examine the roles of marital status and children on the elderly's housing changes. Reschovsky (1990) finds that married home-owners tend to have less to gain by moving from their homes or switching tenure. Feinstein and McFadden find that the exit of a wife from a male-headed owning household has a large positive effect on the household's mobility, and a negative (but insignificant) effect on a moving household's propensity to remain an owner. Similar results are found by Venti and Wise (1989).

In addition, many studies have found that being married greatly reduces the elderly's chances of institutionalization. (See Garber and MaCurdy (1989), Ellwood and Kane (1989), and Boersch-Supan (1989), among others.) Having a spouse also tends to reduce the propensity to live dependently with others or with children. (See Kotlikoff and Morris (1988), and Boersch-Supan (1989).)

Children also seem to have an effect on the elderly's housing decisions. Venti and Wise (1990) find that the presence of children deters owners from moving. Feinstein and McFadden (1987) report that the change in the number of children in a household is negatively related with both the elderly's mobility and the mobile homeowner's propensity to remain an owner. This result could be interpreted to mean that children leaving the home tend to increase mobility but also to increase moves to other owner-occupied dwellings.

As would be expected, Boersch-Supan, Kotlikoff, and Morris (1988) find that the number of parent's offspring both increases the likelihood that they live with their children and reduces their propensity to live with others as a dependent. Similar, although weaker evidence can be found in Boersch-Supan (1989).

Other Factors

The onset of retirement may also cause elderly home-owners to decide to leave their homes. Not having a job reduces the costs of a location change, and the date of retirement may mark the beginning of the household's desire to dissave, possibly out of home equity.

Several authors have examined the relationship between retirement and housing change. Venti and Wise (1989) report that being retired tends to increase elderly homeowners' mobility. Feinstein and McFadden (1987) concur, and also find that the same relationship holds for wives' retirement status. Venti and Wise (1989) also find that changes in retirement status (whether it is becoming retired or coming out of retirement), increase elderly homeowners' mobility. Feinstein and McFadden (1987) find that the head of house-hold being retired also makes it more likely that owners become renters.

Gender may also play a role in the decision to reduce housing equity. Female heads of households may have fewer resources to draw on than male counterparts, and they may be less comfortable in performing routine maintenance. They may also be more likely to move in with independent children.

Reschovsky (1990) notes some correlation between female headship and the potential gains from switching tenure or moving to other owner-occupied housing. This suggests that women may be more likely to reduce their home equity by moving. In general the literature agrees that female heads are less likely to enter an institution. (See Boersch-Supan (1989), and Garber and MaCurdy (1989).) However while

Boersch-Supan (1989) finds evidence that female heads are less likely to live with their children or others as a dependent, Kotlikoff and Morris (1988) report that elderly females are more likely to live with their children.

SUMMARY

As the length of the previous sections attest, many factors play a role in the complex housing decisions of elderly homeowners. Some factors involve financial considerations such as wealth and income, while others are demographic in nature. While there has been much work dedicated to the subject, there are still many areas that remain unclear. In particular, the effect of the value of the homeowners' home equity and other assets on their housing decisions remain essentially unexplored. Also, the transition from home ownership to dependency has not been isolated from all types of moves to dependency. Finally, while both financial and demographic effects on housing decisions has been examined, in general they are not treated simultaneously.

In this work some light is shed on these areas of concern. The following chapters will provide a unified framework for the exploration of the financial, demographic, and other factors that determine the housing decisions of elderly homeowners.

APPENDIX A

A nontrivial number of older households actually do take out new mortgages on their homes. This occurs in spite of the fact that it may be an unusual investment decision for the elderly: The acquisition of a new mortgage on one's home is a way to dissave out of home equity in the short term, but it is also a commitment to build home equity as the mortgage matures. Thus, as the mortgage matures it forces the household to save, the opposite of what it might wish to do.

Using contemporary interest rates, it appears that investing the proceeds of a new mortgage while paying it off will not provide substantial income. As an illustrative example, let's consider a 70 year-old homeowner who reduces home equity by acquiring a 30-year, $80,000 mortgage on her $100,000 home. For argument's sake, let's say that the homeowner knows that she will die at age 85, and has no bequest motive. Let us also assume that the homeowner can put the proceeds of the mortgage in investments that yield the rate of return of 1-year certificates of deposit, and that the mortgage rate is that of a conventional, existing-home mortgage. In 1988, these rates were 7.47% and 10.31% respectively. (Source: *Statistical Abstract of the U.S. (1990)*).

The mortgage payments under these terms would be approximately $8,640 per year. An $80,000 fund that gradually liquidated itself in 15 years would provide a yearly income supplement of $8,868. This investment strategy would thus provide only about $228 per year. Net tax advantages are unlikely to be more than a few hundred dollars per year. There is also reason to believe that this overstates the benefits: The gap between the interest rates was its smallest ever in 1988, and the risk that the homeowner may live longer than age 85 is ignored.

NOTES

[1] It is unclear why reverse mortgages are not more popular. some explanations: (1) Only recently has the federal tax code been amended to define the tax treatment of income from reverse mortgages. (2) Adverse selection and moral hazard problems caused financial institutions to put unacceptable provisions on their first contracts. (3) older homeowners simply do not know enough about reverse mortgages. For a complete discussion consult Scholen and Chen (1980).

[2] The initial cost of a mortgage may include origination fees, title searches, insurance, and recording fees.

[3] Of course the size and quality of the housing may vary substantially across tenure.

[4] One could criticize these results as somewhat self explanatory: Those households that have more positive attitudes toward home ownership will almost by definition be more satisfied with their homes.

II. A MATHEMATICAL MODEL

This chapter presents a mathematical model of the housing decisions of elderly homeowners. The model attempts to capture the factors that are most important in determining an elderly homeowner's housing decision. The factors considered include the homeowner's home equity, financial assets, income, housing cost, and psychological attachment[1] to the home. Although many empirical studies have examined these factors, few have treated them theoretically and none have integrated all of them into a single framework. The theory presented here is similar to earlier work by Artle and Varaiya (1978). It is different because it concentrates only on the aged, explicitly includes preference for home ownership, and treats tenure choice endogenously.

The aim of the chapter is to derive testable hypotheses regarding the effect of various factors on homeowners' propensity to undertake various housing changes. The hypotheses will serve to motivate and guide the empirical chapters that follow.

ASSUMPTIONS AND NOTATION

The analysis begins by considering an elderly household currently at time 0 with certain time of death T. The household receives instantaneous utility from ordinary consumption and from the amount of owner-occupied housing owned. It is assumed that the utility function is separable in these two goods, and can be written for any time $t < T$ as:

$$(2.1) \qquad U(C_t) + \mathcal{H}_t \cdot \phi_t$$

where C_t is ordinary consumption at time t; $\mathcal{H}_t$ is the amount of housing owned at time t, (assumed to remain constant unless a housing change is made); $U(\cdot)$ is the utility function on ordinary consumption, (with $U'(\cdot) > 0$ and $U''(\cdot) < 0$); and ϕ_t represents the household's preference for owner-occupied housing, which is assumed to decline through time: $(\phi_t = \phi_0 - \lambda t)$.[2]

The household begins with an endowment of financial assets A_0, and an initial level of home equity H_0, on which there is no mortgage debt. These amounts appreciate at real rates of return r_a and r_h respectively. The household receives a fixed income (I), and pays constant out-of-pocket housing costs (p_0) at each moment. The household's budget constraint can then be written as:

$$(2.2) \qquad \dot{H}_t + \dot{A}_t \; = \; I - C_t + r_a(A_t) + r_h(H_t) - p_0 \qquad .$$

Please note that $\mathcal{H}$ and H are not the same variable, indicating that amount of housing and its equity are not defined to be equal: They will vary across time due to appreciation of the home equity.

For the time being, the household is also restricted from choosing to live in an owner-occupied home without holding its full value as home equity. The restriction is necessary to prevent the household from choosing $\mathcal{H}_t > 0$ and $H_t = 0$, which would allow the homeowner to sell the home without moving from it. (This restriction will be relaxed in a later section to allow the owner to acquire a mortgage on the home without moving.) The restriction is written mathematically as:

$$(2.3) \qquad\qquad H_t \: / \: \exp[r_h t] \; = \; \mathcal{H}_t \cdot h$$

where h is a scaling factor relating the amount of home equity to the corresponding amount of owner-occupied housing. Without loss of generality h is set equal to 1. Please note that (2.3) does not restrict the household from (simultaneously) changing their levels of H_t and $\mathcal{H}_t$ at various times, merely that the two terms maintain a (changing) proportional relationship with each other at any given time.

It is also necessary to have a restriction on the level of financial assets held, otherwise the household might borrow an infinite amount ($A_t = -\infty$) and consume it to maximize utility. Requiring terminal assets to be nonnegative ($A_T \geq 0$) would solve the problem, but it would allow the household to hold negative financial assets up to the amount of home equity, and then an instant before death repay the debt by selling the home. This strategy is essentially a reverse mortgage, and, as discussed in the previous chapter, has not been an available alternative for most households. Thus the household is required to hold nonnegative financial assets at all times:

(2.4) $$A_t \geq 0 \quad \forall t$$.

The household is also assumed to have a bequest function, and that the contribution of bequests to lifetime utility depends on the amount of financial assets and housing held at the date of death: $B(A_T, \mathcal{H}_T)$.

Should the household choose to make a housing change, it will bear a psychological cost of moving ξ. To simplify the analysis it is assumed that ξ is large enough to make multiple housing changes between 0 and T non-optimal.

Given restrictions (2.2), (2.3), and (2.4), the household will maximize its continuous-time discounted utility by choosing C_t and $\mathcal{H}_t$ over the rest of its lifetime:

(2.5) $$\max_{C_t, \mathcal{H}_t} \int_0^T e^{-\delta t} U(C_t) dt + \int_0^T e^{-\delta t} (\mathcal{H}_t \cdot \phi_t) dt$$

$$- e^{-\delta t} (\xi \cdot E_t) + e^{-\delta T} B(A_T, \mathcal{H}_T)$$

$$\text{s.t.} \quad \dot{H}_t + \dot{A}_t = I - C_t + r_a(A_t) + r_h(H_t) - p_o$$
$$H_t / \exp[r_h t] = \mathcal{H}_t$$
$$A_t \geq 0 \quad \forall t$$

where δ is the household's rate of time preference, and E_t equals 1 if the household makes a housing change in time t, 0 if not.

EXPRESSIONS FOR NO CHANGE

This section derives an expression for the utility that a household receives if it makes no housing changes between times 0 and T, (i.e. $\mathcal{H}_t = \mathcal{H}_0 \ \forall t$). Later sections will derive expressions for the utility associated with various types of housing changes. Comparative statics are then derived.

For any period that the household does not make an active change in their home equity, the actual change will be $r_h(H_t)$. Using this and equation (2.2), the following expression is derived:

$$(2.6) \qquad \dot{A}_t = I - C_t + r_a(A_t) - p_o$$

which is the household's budget constraint for times when no equity change occurs. Rearrangement yields an expression for consumption in every such instant:

$$(2.7) \qquad C_t = I - p_o + r_a(A_t) - \dot{A}_t \qquad .$$

For simplicity, it is assumed that the rate of interest is such that (ceteris paribus) consumption will be the same amount for all t. (See Yaari (1964).)[3] Because it is assumed that I and p_o are also constant through time, the amount "dissaved"[4] in any instant (the last two terms of (2.7)) will also be a constant. Therefore the instantaneous change in the level of financial assets can be expressed as a simple first order differential equation:

$$(2.8) \qquad \dot{A}_t = r_a(A_t) - z_n$$

where z_n is the constant amount dissaved in any instant. The solution to equation (2.8) is:

$$(2.9) \qquad A_t = A_0 \cdot \exp[r_a t] - \frac{z_n}{r_a} \cdot (\exp[r_a t] - 1)$$

Solving this equation for z_n when t = T yields:

$$(2.10) \qquad z_n = \frac{(A_0 \cdot \exp[r_a T] - A_{TN}) \cdot r_a}{(\exp[r_a T] - 1)}$$

where A_{TN} is the terminal asset level. With the use of equation (2.8), the household's consumption can be expressed as:

$$(2.11) \qquad C_t = I - p_o + z_n \qquad .$$

Given this expression for consumption, and knowing that $\mathcal{H}_t = \mathcal{H}_0 \; \forall t$, expression (2.5) can be used to write the expression for utility when no housing change is made between 0 and T:

$$(2.12) \quad \int_0^T e^{-\delta t} U(I - p_o + z_n) dt \;+\; \int_0^T e^{-\delta t} (\mathcal{H}_0 \cdot (\phi_0 - \lambda t)) dt$$

$$+ \; e^{-\delta T} B(A_{TN}, \mathcal{H}_0) \qquad .$$

Should the household decide to remain in their home until T, it can maximize its utility merely by selecting the optimal level of terminal assets (A_{TN}). The selection of A_{TN} will uniquely define z_n and therefore expression (2.12).

EXPRESSIONS FOR HOUSING CHANGES

This section explains the derivation of expressions analogous to (2.12) for several housing changes: (1) Complete home equity liquidation; (2) partial home equity liquidation; (3) an increase in the amount of home equity held; and (4) acquisition of a mortgage. As mentioned above it is assumed that psychological transaction costs are large enough to discourage multiple changes. Although examination of multiple housing changes by the same household is possible, it is not very fruitful. Thus the analysis is limited to situations involving only one housing change.

Complete Liquidation of Home Equity
The simplest housing change to describe is the complete liquidation of home equity. The homeowner could accomplish this by selling the home and moving to a rental unit, moving in with relatives, entering a nursing home, or switching to

a number of other alternative living arrangements. The proceeds of the sale of the home would provide the household with a source of extra consumption, but after the sale the household would no longer enjoy the benefits of home ownership.

Should the household decide to undertake one of the above housing changes, it will do so at some time t_L^*. Therefore, $\mathcal{H}_t$ will be equal to $\mathcal{H}_0$ until time t_L^*, and will be equal to zero after:

$$(2.13) \qquad \mathcal{H}_t = \mathcal{H}_0 \qquad 0 < t < t_L^*$$
$$= 0 \qquad t_L^* \leq t < T \qquad .$$

Similarly, the household will hold the appreciated value of its home equity until t_L^*, and will hold no home equity after:

$$(2.14) \qquad H_t = H_0 \cdot \exp[r_h t] \qquad 0 < t < t_L^*$$
$$= 0 \qquad t_L^* \leq t < T \qquad .$$

Thus equation (2.6) will hold in every instant except at the time of liquidation t_L^*. At that time the amount $H_0 \cdot \exp[r_h t_L^*]$ is added to the existing amount of assets. Thus separate expressions are needed to describe the amount of dissaving that occurs before and after home equity liquidation. Utilizing the techniques used to derive (2.10), the following expressions for the pre- and post-liquidation dissaving are constructed:

$$(2.15) \quad z_{bL} = \frac{(A_0 \cdot \exp[r_a t_L^*] - A_{Lt*}) \cdot r_a}{(\exp[r_a t_L^*] - 1)} \qquad \text{and}$$

$$(2.16) \quad z_{aL}' = \frac{[(A_{Lt*} + H_0 \cdot \exp[r_h t_L^*])\exp[r_a(T-t_L^*)] - A_{LT}] \cdot r_a}{(\exp[r_a(T-t_L^*)] - 1)}$$

where A_{Lt*} is the level of assets chosen at t_L^* when the household decides to liquidate home equity, and A_{LT} is the terminal level of assets if the household liquidates home equity.

To express the change in consumption after the liquidation, expression (2.16) must be altered to account for the change in the out-of-pocket cost of housing:

$$(2.17) \quad z_{aL} =$$

$$\frac{[(A_{Lt*}+H_0 \cdot \exp[r_h t_L^*])\exp[r_a(T-t_L^*)] - A_{LT}] \cdot r_a}{(\exp[r_a(T-t_L^*)] - 1} + p_o - p_L$$

where p_L represents the out-of-pocket cost of alternative housing. The household's utility in the case of complete home equity liquidation at time t_L^* can then be expressed as:

$$(2.18) \quad \int_0^{t_L^*} e^{-\delta t} U(I-p_o+z_{bL})dt + \int_{t_L^*}^T e^{-\delta t} U(I-p_o+z_{aL})dt$$

$$+ \int_0^{t_L^*} e^{-\delta t}(\mathcal{H}_0 \cdot (\phi_0 - \lambda t))dt - e^{-\delta t_L} \cdot \xi + e^{-\delta T}B(A_{LT},0) \, .$$

Should the household decide to completely liquidate their home equity at the optimal time t_L^*, it can maximize its utility by selecting the optimal level of terminal assets given liquidation (A_{LT}), and the optimal level of assets at time t_L^* given liquidation (A_{Lt*}). The selection of these two asset levels will uniquely define z_{bL} and z_{aL} and therefore expression (2.18).

Partial Reduction of Home Equity
The household need not completely liquidate home equity to finance extra consumption. A partial reduction in home equity by moving to an owner-occupied house of lesser value would provide some funds to increase consumption and still allow the household to enjoy some benefits of home ownership.

If the household decides to move to another owner-occupied home of lesser value, it will do so at a time denoted t_p^*. Under these circumstances, $\mathcal{H}_t$ will be equal to

$\mathcal{H}_0$ until time t_P^*, and will equal some optimal post-move amount of housing ($\mathcal{H}_P$) after t_P^*:

(2.19) $\mathcal{H}_t = \mathcal{H}_0 \qquad 0 < t < t_P^*$

                          $\quad\; = \mathcal{H}_P \qquad t_P^* \leq t < T$.

Likewise, the household will hold its original appreciated value of home equity until t_P^*, and will hold an appreciating smaller amount after t_P^*:

(2.20) $H_t = H_0 \cdot \exp[r_h t] \qquad\quad 0 < t < t_P^*$

                 $\quad\; = H_P \cdot \exp[r_h(t-t_P^*)] \qquad t_P^* \leq t < T$

where H_P is the smaller level of home equity chosen at t_P^*.

Recall restriction (2.3) and note that H_P and $\mathcal{H}_P$ are governed by the relationship

(2.21) $H_P \,/\, \exp[r_h t_P^*] \,=\, \mathcal{H}_P$.

This restriction requires the household to reduce home equity in proportion to its reduction in owner-occupied housing, after appreciation of home equity is accounted for. (A similar condition exists for the case of complete liquidation, but it is trivial since both H_p and $\mathcal{H}_p$ are equal to 0.) Equation (2.21) has the effect of not allowing the household to choose high values of $\mathcal{H}_P$ while simultaneously choosing low values of H_P.

As in the previous section, equation (2.6) will hold in every instant except at the time of equity reduction t_P^*. At that time the amount ($H_0 \cdot \exp[r_h t_P^*] - H_P$) is added to the existing amount of assets. The expressions describing the dissaving that occurs before and after a partial reduction in home equity are:

(2.22) $z_{bP} = \dfrac{(A_0 \cdot \exp[r_a t_P^*] - A_{Pt*}) \cdot r_a}{(\exp[r_a t_P^*] - 1)}$ and

(2.23) $z'_{aP} = \dfrac{[(A_{Pt*} + H_0 \cdot \exp[r_h t_P^*] - H_P)\exp[r_a(T-t_P^*)] - A_{PT}] \cdot r_a}{(\exp[r_a(T-t_P^*)] - 1)}$

where A_{Pt*} is the level of assets chosen at t_P^* when the household decides to partially reduce home equity, and A_{PT} is the terminal level of assets if the household partially reduces home equity.

To arrive at the expression for the amount of extra consumption derived from partial equity reduction, the post-change dissaving expression must be adjusted to reflect the change in out-of-pocket housing costs:

(2.24) z_{aP} =

$$\frac{[(A_{Pt*}+H_0 \cdot \exp[r_h\, t_P^*]-H_P)\exp[r_a(T-t_P^*)]-A_{PT}] \cdot r_a}{(\exp[r_a(T-t_P^*)] - 1)} + p_o - p_P$$

where p_P represents the out-of-pocket housing costs after the household moves to a home of lesser value. The utility from partial home equity reduction at time t_P^* can then be expressed as:

(2.25)
$$\int_0^{t_P^*} e^{-\delta t}\, U(I-p_o+z_{bP})dt \;+\; \int_{t_P^*}^{T} e^{-\delta t}\, U(I-p_o+z_{aP})dt$$

$$+ \int_0^{t_P^*} e^{-\delta t}(\mathcal{H}_0 \cdot (\phi_0-\lambda t))dt \;+\; \int_{t_P^*}^{T} e^{-\delta t}(\mathcal{H}_P \cdot (\phi_0-\lambda t))dt$$

$$- e^{-\delta t_P^*} \cdot \xi \;+\; e^{-\delta T}B(A_{PT},\mathcal{H}_P) \qquad .$$

If the household decides to partially reduce its home equity at the optimal time t_P^*, it will maximize expression (2.25) by choosing an optimal lower level of housing ($\mathcal{H}_P$), (and therefore H_P by expression (2.21)), an optimal level of assets at time t_P^* given partial reduction (A_{Pt*}), and the optimal level of terminal assets given partial reduction (A_{PT}). Choosing these three values uniquely defines expressions (2.22) and (2.24) and therefore defines expression (2.25).

Increase in Home Equity

Of course reducing or liquidating home equity is not the only alternative for current homeowners. Under some circumstances, it may be optimal for a household to increase its home equity by moving to a home of greater value than the current home. A move of this type increases the amount of owner-occupied housing that the homeowner enjoys, but decreases the funds available for consumption expenditures.

This alternative can be described along the lines of the previous subsections. If a household decides to increase home equity by moving to a home of greater value, it will do so at some time t_I^*. Under these circumstances, $\mathcal{H}_t$ will be equal to $\mathcal{H}_0$ until time t_I^*, and will equal some optimal post-move amount of housing $(\mathcal{H}_I)$ after t_I^*:

$$(2.26) \qquad \mathcal{H}_t = \mathcal{H}_0 \qquad 0 < t < t_I^*$$
$$= \mathcal{H}_I \qquad t_I^* \le t < T \qquad .$$

Analogously to the previous subsection, the amount of home equity held through time can be described by:

$$(2.27) \qquad H_t = H_0 \cdot \exp[r_h t] \qquad 0 < t < t_I^*$$
$$= H_I \cdot \exp[r_h(t-t_I^*)] \qquad t_I^* \le t < T$$

and H_I and $\mathcal{H}_I$ will be related to one another by the following equation:

$$(2.28) \qquad H_I / \exp[r_h t_I^*] = \mathcal{H}_I$$

Equation (2.6) will be true in every instant except at time t_I^*. At that moment $(H_I - H_0 \cdot \exp[r_h t])$ will be subtracted from the existing amount of assets to finance the increase in home equity. The dissaving that occurs before and after the increase in home equity can be expressed as:

$$(2.29) \quad z_{bI} = \frac{(A_0 \cdot \exp[r_a t_I^*] - A_{I t*}) \cdot r_a}{(\exp[r_a t_I^*] - 1)} \qquad \text{and}$$

$$(2.30) \quad z_{aI}' = \frac{[(A_{It*} + H_0 \cdot \exp[r_h t_I^*] - H_I) \exp[r_a(T-t_I^*)] - A_{IT}] \cdot r_a}{(\exp[r_a(T-t_I^*)] - 1)}$$

where A_{It*} is the level of assets chosen at t_I^* if the household decides to increase home equity by moving, and A_{IT} is the terminal level of assets when such a move occurs.

Adjusting (2.30) by including the difference in out-of-pocket costs from the housing change yields:

(2.31) $\quad z_{aI} \; = $

$$\frac{[(A_{It*}+H_0 \cdot \exp[r_h t_I^*]-H_I)\exp[r_a(T-t_I^*)]-A_{IT}] \cdot r_a}{(\exp[r_a(T-t_I^*)] \; - \; 1)} \; + \; p_o - p_I$$

where p_I is the out-of-pocket housing cost of the home of greater value. The utility from increasing home equity by moving at time t_I^* can be expressed as:

$$(2.32) \quad \int_0^{t_I^*} e^{-\delta t} U(I-p_o+z_{bI})dt \; + \; \int_{t_I^*}^T e^{-\delta t} U(I-p_o+z_{aI})dt$$

$$+ \; \int_0^{t_I^*} e^{-\delta t}(\mathscr{H}_0 \cdot (\phi_0 - \lambda t))dt \; + \; \int_{t_I^*}^T e^{-\delta t}(\mathscr{H}_I \cdot (\phi_0 - \lambda t))dt$$

$$- \; e^{-\delta t_I^*} \cdot \xi \; + \; e^{-\delta T}B(A_{IT}, \mathscr{H}_I) \qquad .$$

If the household chooses to increase its home equity by moving to another home at time t_I^*, it will do so by choosing an optimal greater level of housing ($\mathscr{H}_I$, an optimal level of assets at time t_I^* (A_{It*}), and an optimal level of terminal assets given the increase in home equity (A_{IT}). Choosing these values uniquely defines expression (2.32) via expressions (2.28), (2.29) and (2.31).

Acquisition of a Mortgage
The final housing change explored in this chapter is the acquisition of a new mortgage on the presently occupied home. Mortgaging one's home may be an attractive way of utilizing home equity because it allows a household to utilize the value of the home to finance extra consumption

without incurring the psychological and transaction costs of moving. However acquiring a new mortgage also has some disadvantages: High finance charges from the mortgage will reduce the supplemental consumption from the proceeds of the loan; and the level of home equity held by the household will gradually increase, rather than decrease, as the mortgage is paid off.

As with the baseline (no change) alternative described above, the amount of housing held by a homeowner who chooses to acquire a mortgage will remain constant between 0 and T: ($\mathcal{H}_t = \mathcal{H}_0 \ \forall t$). However home equity will take a more complicated path, and it will no longer conform to equation (2.3). It will initially increase at rate r_h, just as it does in the other alternatives, until time t_M^*, the date that the household acquires a new mortgage. At t_M^*, home equity will fall by the amount of home equity that is mortgaged, $k \cdot (H_0 \cdot \exp[r_h t_M^*])$, where k is the percentage of home equity at time t_M^* that is mortgaged. After t_M^*, home equity will increase by the amount of appreciation on the entire value of home equity plus the amount of principle that is paid off in any instant. The path is summarized in the following equations:

$$(2.33) \quad H_t = H_0 \cdot \exp[r_h t] \qquad 0 < t < t_M^*$$
$$\quad = H_0 \cdot \exp[r_h t] - M_t \qquad t_M^* \leq t < T$$

where M_t is the amount of mortgage principle owed at time t and can be expressed by:

$$(2.34) \quad M_t = [k \cdot H_0 \cdot \exp[r_h t_M^*]] \ \cdot$$

$$\left[\exp[r_m(t-t_M^*)] - \frac{\exp[r_m(T_M-t_M^*)] \cdot (\exp[r_m(t-t_M^*)]-1)}{\exp[r_m(T_M-t_M^*)]-1} \right]$$

where T_M denotes the date that the mortgage is paid off, which may be before or after the date of death T.

As in the previous subsections, equation (2.6) will hold at every instant except at t_M^*, when the amount $(k \cdot H_0 \cdot \exp[r_h t_M^*])$ is added to the existing level of assets.

It is also assumed that acquiring the mortgage costs a one-time fixed amount F. The amount of dissaving before and after the acquisition of the mortgage can then be written as follows:

$$(2.35) \quad z_{bM} = \frac{(A_0 \cdot \exp[r_a t_M^*] - A_{Mt*}) \cdot r_a}{(\exp[r_a t_M^*] - 1)} \quad \text{and}$$

$$(2.36) \quad z_{aM}' = \frac{[(A_{Mt*} + kH_0 \exp[r_h t_M^*] - F) \exp[r_a (T - t_M^*)] - A_{MT}] \cdot r_a}{(\exp[r_a (T - t_M^*)] - 1)}$$

where A_{Mt*} is the optimal asset level at time t_M^* if a new mortgage is acquired, and A_{MT} is the optimal level of assets at the date of death should a new mortgage be obtained.

In order to adjust (2.36) to represent consumption after the mortgage is acquired, note that p_0 will still be paid (and thus does not appear), and an additional mortgage payment (p_M) should be subtracted. Consumption after the mortgage is acquired can therefore be expressed by:

$$(2.37) \quad z_{aM} =$$
$$\frac{[(A_{Mt*} + kH_0 \exp[r_h t_M^*] - F) \exp[r_a (T - t_M^*)] - A_{MT}] \cdot r_a}{(\exp[r_a (T - t_M^*)] - 1)} - p_M \quad .$$

The expression for the amount of the mortgage payment (p_M) is found by solving the differential equation that describes the movement of remaining mortgage principal. Doing so yields:

$$(2.38) \quad p_M = \frac{[k \cdot H_0 \cdot \exp[r_h t_M^*] \cdot \exp[r_m (T_M - t_M^*)] \cdot r_m]}{\exp[r_m (T_M - t_M^*)] - 1} \quad .$$

The expression for the utility of a household that decides to acquire a new mortgage at time t_M^* can then be expressed as:

$$(2.39) \quad \int_{0}^{t_M^*} e^{-\delta t} \, U(I-p_o+z_{bM})dt \; + \; \int_{t_M^*}^{T} e^{-\delta t} \, U(I-p_o+z_{aM})dt$$

$$+ \int_{0}^{T} e^{-\delta t}(\mathcal{H}_0 \cdot (\phi_0 - \lambda t))dt \; + \; e^{-\delta T}B(A_{MT}-M_T, \mathcal{H}_0)$$

where M_T is the remaining mortgage principal owed at the time of death, and is defined by expression (2.34). It appears in the bequest function as being subtracted from the terminal level of assets.

Should the household choose to acquire a mortgage at the optimal choice of time t_M^*, it will maximize expression (2.39) by choosing A_{Mt^*}, the level of financial assets at t_M^*; A_{MT}, the level of financial assets at the time of death; and M_T, the amount of outstanding mortgage principle at the time of death. The household's choice of M_T, (along with market-defined r_m and T_M) defines k via equation (2.34). Using k, A_{Mt^*}, and A_{MT}, expressions (2.35) and (2.37) are defined and thus uniquely define (2.39).

No doubt the reader has noticed that expressions (2.18), (2.25), (2.32), and (2.39) share a similar form and are derived in a similar manner. Indeed one could think of these expressions as being particular examples of a more general expression that allows the homeowner to choose over all housing alternatives (and all $\mathcal{H}_t$) in any period to maximize utility. The separate expressions are explicitly stated because in later sections each will be used to calculate comparative statics that vary across alternatives.

It may be possible to describe other sorts of housing changes, such as taking other people into the home to share expenses, moving from a smaller to a larger home by acquiring a mortgage on the new home, or allowing home maintenance to go undone, thereby saving money that could be used for consumption. A particularly inviting extension would be to allow households to move to locations where a given amount of home equity buys a greater amount of owner-occupied housing. For the time being the analysis is limited to the previously mentioned housing changes as the available alternatives for elderly homeowners.

EXPRESSIONS FOR UTILITY GAIN
AND COMPARATIVE STATICS

In the previous section expressions for the utility that a household receives under different housing changes are derived. In this section the conditions under which these changes will actually occur are examined, as well as the factors that affect the decision to make the changes. The section begins by examining expressions that describe the gain in utility from making each of the previously described housing changes. Then with the use of partial differentiation, comparative statics are derived.

The Gain from Liquidation

An expression for the gain from home equity liquidation can be found by subtracting expression (2.12) from expression (2.18). By splitting the integral in expression (2.12) and recombining terms, the following expression is derived:

$$(2.40) \quad \int_0^{t_L^*} e^{-\delta t} \left[U(I-p_o+z_{hL}) - U(I-p_o+z_n) \right] dt$$

$$+ \int_{t_L^*}^T e^{-\delta t} \left[U(I-p_o+z_{aL}) - U(I-p_o+z_n) \right] dt$$

$$- \int_{t_L^*}^T e^{-\delta t} (\mathcal{H}_0 \cdot (\phi_0 - \lambda t)) dt - e^{-\delta t_L^*} \cdot \xi$$

$$+ e^{-\delta T} [B(A_{LT}, 0) - B(A_{NT}, \mathcal{H}_0)] \quad .$$

Evaluating the integrals and taking second order Taylor approximations around the z terms yields:

$$(2.41) \quad G_L = \frac{1 - \exp(-\delta t_L^*)}{\delta} \cdot$$

$$\left[(z_{bL} - z_n) \cdot U'(I - p_o) + \frac{(z_{bL})^2 - (z_n)^2}{2} \cdot U''(I - p_o) \right]$$

$$+ \frac{[\exp(-\delta t_L^*) - \exp(-\delta T)]}{\delta} \cdot$$

$$\left[(z_{aL} - z_n) \cdot U'(I - p_o) + \frac{(z_{aL})^2 - (z_n)^2}{2} \cdot U''(I - p_o) \right]$$

$$- \frac{\mathcal{H}_0}{\delta} \left[\exp(-\delta t_L^*) \cdot [\phi_0 - \lambda t_L^* - \lambda/\delta] - \exp(-\delta T) \cdot [\phi_0 - \lambda T - \lambda/\delta] \right]$$

$$- \xi [\exp(-\delta t_L^*)] + e^{-\delta T} [B(A_{LT}, 0) - B(A_{NT}, \mathcal{H}_0)] \quad .$$

In expression (2.41), the first line represents the utility gain between 0 and t_L^* from the extra consumption made possible by the future home equity liquidation. The second and third lines represent the utility gain between t_L^* and T from the extra consumption after home equity is liquidated. The fourth line represents the forgone utility from not owning any owner-occupied housing from t_L^* to T; and the last line is the loss in utility due to the housing change, and the difference in utility from bequests.

The expression for G_L may be positive or negative depending on the values of the underlying parameters. It will attain its greatest value at the optimal value t_L^*, and if $G_L | t_L^* > 0$, the household may liquidate home equity at that time.

Comparative Statics for Liquidation

At this point expression (2.41) remains general in the sense that the z terms need not be positive. (i.e. the household can either be saving or dissaving between 0 and T). However, to evaluate the signs of the comparative statics below it is assumed that $z_{bL}, z_{aL} > z_n > 0$; that is, the elderly do dissave out of financial assets and they dissave more if they liquidate home equity.

Because t_L^*, A_{Lt*}, A_{NT}, and A_{LT} are all defined as choice variables, the envelope theorem applies to them when perorming comparative statics. This is a tremendous help when determining the signs of the derivatives. Differentiating expression (2.41) with respect to certain variables yields a number of interesting relationships:

$\partial G_L / \partial H_0 > 0$ A higher initial value of home equity means that the home will be worth more when sold, and thus provide greater increased consumption.

$\partial G_L / \partial A_0 < 0$ The utility from an extra unit of initial financial assets is greater when the household does not choose to liquidate home equity. An extra amount of assets will increase consumption in both the liquidation and no liquidation cases, but it will be more valuable in utility terms in the no liquidation case due to diminishing marginal utility. Intuitively, greater financial wealth makes equity liquidation less necessary to sustain consumption.

$\partial G_L / \partial I < 0$ The greater a household's income the less need they have to supplement it with liquidated home equity.

$\partial G_L / \partial p_o > 0$ The higher the cost of owner-occupied housing, the more attractive alternative housing arrangements are.

$\partial G_L / \partial p_L < 0$ The higher the cost of alternative housing, the less attractive home equity liquidation seems.

$\partial G_L / \partial \phi_0 < 0$ The greater the initial utility from each unit of owner-occupied housing owned, the less gain one will receive from leaving it.

$\partial G_L / \partial \lambda > 0$ The faster the deterioration in a household's preference for home ownership, the greater the gain in utility from equity liquidation.

To the extent that these relationships represent increases or decreases in the gain from liquidating home equity, they will also represent increases or decreases in a household's propensity to liquidate home equity by leaving the current home for other accommodations. They therefore represent a set of testable hypotheses.

The Gain from Partial Reduction

The expression for the utility gain from partial home equity reduction can be found using the same method used above. First expression (2.12) is subtracted from (2.25). The integrals of (2.12) are then split and their terms are rearranged. After evaluating the integrals, performing second order Taylor approximations and simplifying, the utility gain from partial home equity liquidation is found to be:

$$(2.42) \quad G_P = \frac{[1-\exp(-\delta t_P^*)]}{\delta} \cdot$$

$$\left[(z_{bP}-z_n) \cdot U'(I-p_o) + \frac{(z_{bP})^2-(z_n)^2}{2} \cdot U''(I-p_o) \right]$$

$$+ \frac{[\exp(-\delta t_P^*)-\exp(-\delta T)]}{\delta} \cdot$$

$$\left[(z_{aP}-z_n) \cdot U'(I-p_o) + \frac{(z_{aP})^2-(z_n)^2}{2} \cdot U''(I-p_o) \right]$$

$$- \frac{\mathcal{H}_0-\mathcal{H}_P}{\delta}\left[\exp(-\delta t_P^*)\cdot[\phi_0-\lambda t_P^*-\lambda/\delta] - \exp(-\delta T)\cdot[\phi_0-\lambda T-\lambda/\delta]\right]$$

$$- \xi\,[\exp(-\delta t_P^*)] + e^{-\delta T}[B(A_{PT},\mathcal{H}_P) - B(A_{NT},\mathcal{H}_0)] \quad .$$

Expression (2.42) is very similar to its predecessor describing complete liquidation, and has the same interpretation. Note the difference in the fifth line, which describes the lost utility from not owning the original amount of housing. In (2.42) this line is a smaller negative value due to the fact that some housing is still owned. The expression also differs from (2.41) in that the z terms are a different value, and that the utility from bequests is different.

As in the case of complete liquidation, the expression for G_p may be positive or negative. The household may choose to partially reduce its home equity only if G_p is greater than 0 at time t_P^*.

Comparative Statics for Partial Reduction

The comparative statics for partial home equity reduction are completely analogous to those found in above, (with the exception that ∂p_P should replace ∂p_L), so for the sake of brevity they will not be repeated.

The Gain from an Increase in Home Equity

The expression for the gain in utility from an increase in home equity in the same way as before, this time by subtracting expression (2.12) from (2.32). Performing the mathematical operations described earlier yields the following expression:

$$(2.43) \quad G_I = \frac{[1-\exp(-\delta t_I^*)]}{\delta} \cdot$$

$$\left[(z_{bI}-z_n) \cdot U'(I-p_o) + \frac{(z_{bI})^2-(z_n)^2}{2} \cdot U''(I-p_o) \right]$$

$$+ \frac{[\exp(-\delta t_I^*)-\exp(-\delta T)]}{\delta} \cdot$$

$$\left[(z_{aI}-z_n) \cdot U'(I-p_o) + \frac{(z_{aI})^2-(z_n)^2}{2} \cdot U''(I-p_o) \right]$$

$$- \frac{\mathcal{H}_0-\mathcal{H}_I}{\delta} \left[\exp(-\delta t_I^*) \cdot [\phi_0-\lambda t_I^*-\lambda/\delta] - \exp(-\delta T) \cdot [\phi_0-\lambda T-\lambda/\delta] \right]$$

$$- \xi \, [\exp(-\delta t_I^*)] + e^{-\delta T}[B(A_{IT},\mathcal{H}_I) - B(A_{NT},\mathcal{H}_0)] \quad \cdot$$

Although this expression takes the same form as (2.41) and (2.42), it is different in significant ways. First, it now will be assumed that households who buy houses having more equity will dissave out of financial assets less than those who don't. Mathematically, z_{bI} and z_{aI} will be less than z_n. This means that the expressions for the difference in utility from the change in consumption will now be negative, rather than positive as in expressions (2.41) and (2.42). Also, because $\mathcal{H}_I$ is greater than $\mathcal{H}_0$, the expression for change in utility from housing (the fifth line in (2.42)) will now be positive. These changes will cause a number of differences in the comparative statics described presently.

Comparative Statics for Increase in Home Equity

To evaluate the signs of the following expressions, it is assumed that $z_n > z_{bI}$ and $z_{aI} > 0$; that is, that the elderly dissave out of financial assets even when they purchase a more expensive home, but that they dissave less than if no housing change is made. Differentiating expression (2.43) with respect to the variables of interest yields the following empirically testable relationships:

$\partial G_I/\partial H_0 > 0$ This result is somewhat counterintuitive. It occurs because a higher level of initial home equity makes it easier to buy a home of even larger equity without reducing the financial assets that will provide increased consumption.

$\partial G_I/\partial A_0 > 0$ An extra amount of assets will increase consumption in both the equity increase and the no change cases, but it will be more valuable in utility terms in the equity increase case due to diminishing marginal utility. Intuitively, greater financial wealth makes an equity increase easier.

$\partial G_I/\partial I > 0$ The greater a household's income the easier it is to increase home equity without reducing consumption.

$\partial G_I/\partial p_o \gtrless 0$?   Intuition would suggest that original housing that is more expensive would cause homeowners to find alternative housing arrangements. This is true, but the higher initial housing costs also make it more difficult for a household to afford a home with higher equity. It is impossible to determine which factor dominates.

$\partial G_I/\partial p_I < 0$ The higher the cost of the home with higher home equity, the less attractive the option seems.

$\partial G_I/\partial \phi_0 > 0$ The greater the initial utility from each unit of owner-occupied housing, the more the household has to gain by increasing the amount of housing.

$\partial G_I/\partial \lambda < 0$ The faster the deterioration in a household's preference for home ownership, the smaller the gain in utility from increasing the amount of housing owned.

The Gain from Mortgage Acquisition

To derive the expression describing the utility gain from acquiring a new mortgage, expression (2.12) is first subtracted from (2.39). After splitting the integral in (2.12), evaluating all the integrals, and performing a second order Taylor approximation around the z terms, the following expression is obtained:

$$(2.44) \quad G_M = \frac{[1-\exp(-\delta t_M^*)]}{\delta} \cdot$$

$$\left[(z_{bM}-z_n) \cdot U'(I-p_o) + \frac{(z_{bM})^2-(z_n)^2}{2} \cdot U''(I-p_o) \right]$$

$$+ \frac{[\exp(-\delta t_M^*)-\exp(-\delta T)]}{\delta} \cdot$$

$$\left[(z_{aM}-z_n) \cdot U'(I-p_o) + \frac{(z_{aM})^2-(z_n)^2}{2} \cdot U''(I-p_o) \right]$$

$$+ e^{-\delta T}[B(A_{MT}-M_T,\mathcal{H}_0) - B(A_{NT},\mathcal{H}_0)] \quad .$$

This expression differs from the earlier expressions in that there are no terms the describing the psychological transaction cost or the difference in utility from owning a different amount of housing. Since the household continues to live in the same home, there is no utility cost or change in housing from moving. The financial transaction cost from acquiring a mortgage, F, is embodied in z_{aM}.

As with the preceding utility gain expressions, (2.44) may be either positive or negative. It will attain its greatest value at an optimal time t_M^*. If the expression is positive at that time then the household may acquire a new mortgage.

Comparative Statics for Mortgage Acquisition

For the evaluation of these expressions, assumptions similar to those used previously are adopted. Specifically, z_{bM} and z_{aM} are assumed to be greater than z_n; that is, the household is assumed to dissave at a greater rate if it chooses to acquire a new mortgage. Taking partial derivatives of (2.44) with respect to the variables of interest yields the following:

$\partial G_M / \partial H_0 > 0$ A higher initial value of home equity means that a greater amount of home equity can be mortgaged, thus providing greater increased consumption.

$\partial G_M / \partial A_0 < 0$ An extra amount of assets will increase consumption in both the mortgage acquisition and no change cases, but it will be more valuable in utility terms in the no change case due to diminishing marginal utility. Intuitively, greater financial wealth makes acquiring a new mortgage less necessary to sustain consumption.

$\partial G_M / \partial I < 0$ The greater a household's income the less need they have to supplement it with proceeds from a mortgage.

$\partial G_M/\partial p_o > 0$ The higher the cost of owner-occupied housing, the more valuable the proceeds from a mortgage are.

$\partial G_M/\partial p_m < 0$ The higher the cost of financing the mortgage, the less attractive this alternative will be.

$\partial G_M/\partial \phi_0 = 0$ Because acquiring a new mortgage does not change the amount of housing occupied, any change in the amount that it is enjoyed will have no effect on the gain from acquiring a mortgage.

$\partial G_M/\partial \lambda = 0$ As with ϕ_0, a change in the rate of deterioration of the preference for housing will have no effect on the gain in utility from mortgage acquisition.

These comparative statics are added to the testable hypotheses derived in the previous sections.

SHORTCOMINGS OF THE MODEL

This model, as it stands, is flawed in a number of ways. Most noticeably, it lacks any randomness with respect to utility from home ownership, income, expenses, and time of death. The uncertainty created by unexpected variations of such factors almost certainly has an effect on home-owners' decisions. However, including stochastic elements in the present framework is very burdensome and does not yield tractable results.

The model also suffers from a rather simple treatment of the utility from housing. Specifically, it does not differentiate the utility from various non-owning housing arrangements from one another, (it merely defines ϕ_t as the difference in utility between owner-occupied and all other types of housing), and assumes a linear utility function for owner-occupied housing. However enhancing the model to treat these problems would cause the model to be even more cumbersome and would add little to the understanding of the behavior of interest.

SUMMARY

To the extent that the results of the previous sections represent changes in the utility gain from various housing changes, they will also represent changes in the propensity of homeowners to choose the various alternatives. By observing the actions of homeowners it is possible to estimate the effect of the various factors on the homeowners' propensity to choose the alternatives and thus the utility gain they receive. The results are therefore empirically testable.

The theoretic results of this chapter are summarized in Table 2.1, which describes the effect of various factors on the gain from the housing changes discussed in this chapter. These results are fairly simple and for the most part are intuitive. As the reader can see, the factors have differing effects across the various housing changes. In general financial factors tend to have opposite effects on equity reducing moves compared to equity increasing ones. This suggests that using simple mobility as an indicator of the desire to reduce home equity is inappropriate.

Perhaps the most important result is that for housing changes that reduce home equity, housing wealth and financial wealth will have opposite effects on the utility gains from equity reduction. This suggests that a well-formulated study should disaggregate the two forms of wealth.

Another interesting result is that the comparative statics concerning mortgage acquisition are different from the other equity reducing alternatives. In particular, changes in a household's preference for home ownership will have no effect on the household's desire to acquire a new mortgage relative to making no housing change.Past empirical studies have not been consistent with the theoretic implications of the model. The next chapters seek to provide an empirical treatment consistent with the model described here.

Table 2.1
Summary of Theoretic Results

Change in Utility Gain from Housing Changes
for Increases in Various Factors

Factor	Utility Gain From		
	Equity Reduction/ Liquidation	Equity Increase	Mortgage Acquisition
Home Equity	Increase	Increase	Increase
Financial Assets	Decrease	Increase	Decrease
Income	Decrease	Increase	Decrease
Current Housing Costs	Increase	?	Increase
Alternative Housing Costs	Decrease	Decrease	Decrease
Preference For Home Ownership	Decrease	Increase	0
Reduction in Ownership Preference	Increase	Decrease	0

NOTES

[1] It is assumed that the psychological attachment to the home is a function of marital status, number of children, age, health status, and other demographic characteristics of household members. These factors are not explicitly included in the model, but rather enter implicitly via ϕ_t.

[2] The parameter ϕ_t should be thought of as the difference between the utility of living in owner-occupied housing and the utility from living in non-owner-occupied housing.

[3] This essentially means that $r_a = \delta$. For consumption to be a constant when a home equity change takes place, it must be that $r_h = r_a = \delta$, or another r_h and r_a must be such that the return on the entire wealth portfolio equals δ. Relaxing this assumption would "tilt" consumption by causing the optimal consumption path to grow if $r_a > \delta$, and to fall if $r_a < \delta$. In either case the theoretical results of the chapter should hold, but the complexity of their derivation would be unnecessarily high.

[4] The term "dissaved" is intended to mean that households will consume some amount out of their assets and proceeds from assets. Please note that a household could dissave a positive amount and still have assets growing as long as it dissaved less than $r_a(A_t)$ in any instant. In other words, the level of assets will change by the amount it appreciates minus the amount dissaved.

III. DATA AND INITIAL RESULTS

In this chapter the general characteristics of the data used to study the housing changes of elderly homeowners is examined. The chapter is organized as follows: The first section describes several data sets considered for use in the empirical chapters, and provides a rationale for the one chosen. The next section describes the variables available in the data. Sample selection and data idiosyncrasies are described in a third section. A fourth section provides some descriptive statistics on the elderly's mobility and tenure choice, and a sixth section concentrates on housing transitions of those in owner-occupied housing, and provides some suggestive crosstabulations. The final section discusses the results and summarizes.

The data chosen for analysis comes from the Panel Study of Income Dynamics. The initial results from this data are for the most part consistent with the view that homeowners wish to dissave out of home equity when old. Further results provide mixed evidence for the theoretical predictions regarding financial factors that are contained in chapter 2. Statistical tests consistently indicate that financial variables (home equity, financial assets, housing costs, and income) and demographic variables (marital, employment, and health status) both play roles in elderly homeowners' housing decisions.

DATA SET SELECTION

This section explains the choice of the data set used in this book. Three data sets are examined for their potential in describing and explaining older households' housing behavior. Each data set is discussed and reasons for the choice are made.

The Candidate Data Sets

To undertake an analysis of elderly homeowners' housing decisions a data set is needed that contains sufficient demographic, economic, and housing data on older persons.

Because housing *changes* are of primary interest, the data must also follow its subjects from year to year over a sufficiently long period of time. Three sources of data stand out as candidates when one examines the literature: The Annual Housing Survey (AHS), the Retirement History Survey (RHS), and the Panel Study of Income Dynamics (PSID).

The Annual Housing Survey (or American Housing Survey as it has been called since 1984), is an ongoing study based on nationwide U.S. census data. Its large sample size (over 50,000 in most waves) and extensive information on housing characteristics would be major advantages in any empirical study. Its main drawback is that it does not follow a household after it makes a move, as the survey is actually a panel of structures rather than households. Thus while it can be determined whether the household moved or not, it is impossible to determine the sort of arrangement the household moved to. Also, the AHS is based on the 1970 census for 1974-1983, and is based on the 1980 census after 1983. Thus sampled units are not linked across the 1983-1984 gap, reducing the possible length of any longitudinal study.

Perhaps the most famous of studies on the elderly is the Retirement History Survey. This survey begins in 1969 with 11,153 households with heads aged 58 to 63. It contains data collected biennially in six waves. The RHS contains variables on income, consumption, and asset levels, as well as information describing housing. One of this survey's drawbacks in the context of housing changes is that respondents are only followed for ten years, so that the oldest original respondent is 73 in its last wave. Thus the data would provide no information on the housing transitions of the very old, and may miss transitions that occur after the ten year window of the survey has passed. Another drawback is that measurements occur only every other year, which may obscure multiple housing changes and the timing of changes in crucial variables. Some authors (Hurd (1990), Rust (1989)) have also commented on possible coding errors for some variables.

A less obvious candidate for analysis is the Panel Study of Income Dynamics. Although this study is not a panel of the elderly *per se*, it does include a significant number of the aged. Over 1,400 of the heads of household in the panel are over 50 in its first year (1968). The study is ongoing and data are collected yearly. Income and demographic variables are recorded in each year. Data concerning housing is almost as complete, with the exception that mortgage information is not available in a few of the waves. Variables on financial asset levels are absent in all but one year, although asset income is recorded in each year.

Selection of The Panel Study of Income Dynamics
After reviewing the attributes of each of the data sets, the Panel Study of Income Dynamics was selected for use in this work. The AHS, with its panel of houses rather than occupants, lacks information on the destination of the occupants that move from their houses, and is thus inadequate for the study of housing changes.

Both the RHS and the PSID would be an adequate source of data for this dissertation. Even though the RHS is superior to the PSID when measuring financial assets, the greater length and more frequent observation make the PSID the more attractive candidate.

THE PANEL STUDY OF INCOME DYNAMICS: STRUCTURE AND RELEVANT VARIABLES

This section describes the structure and resources available in the PSID. The organization and characteristics of the study will be explained, as well as variables in the panel that pertain to the study of the elderly's housing decisions.

General Description and Organization
The PSID began in 1968 with information on 18,230 individuals in 4,802 families. Over the 20 year history of the PSID, data has been collected on 37,530 individuals, with thousands of variables recorded for each of them. This makes the individual-level rectangular file rather unwieldy. At the time of the twentieth wave (1987), current respondents numbered 19,578 and came from 7,061 families. The remainder of the 37,530 individuals are contained in newly released nonresponse files. The availability of the nonresponse files is particularly crucial for this work, as

over half the data used in the study are from individuals whose data come from the nonresponse tapes.

Although the number of elderly in the PSID is not nearly the sample size of the RHS or AHS, it is a large enough number to study topics concerning the aged. The structure of the data is rectangular, with successive waves horizontally concatenated onto the existing waves. This structure makes longitudinal study quite easy but is somewhat awkward when pooled cross-sectional analyses are used. Most of the analyses in this work will combine data from two adjacent years to define changes in housing status.

The PSID's individual-level data contains a record for each sample member. Each record is composed of a small number of individual-specific variables and a large number of family variables that are identical for each family member. Thus if one is interested in household-level data one merely has to select a single member from each family.

Housing Variables

The housing variables contained in the PSID are adequate for the present study. In each of the twenty waves respondents are asked whether they own, rent, or have other living arrangements. If they have other arrangements they are asked whether housing is a form of payment for services, is paid for by others, has been sold but they haven't moved out, is temporary quarters, or if they will inherit the housing at some later date. In all of the waves since '68, the household has been asked whether they moved during the past year.

If the household does own their home, its value is recorded in all years. In most years mortgage information (amount of remaining principle, mortgage payment, number of years remaining) is recorded, the exceptions being '68, '73-'75, and '82. In addition to annual mortgage payment, measures of some of the other housing costs are available in most years: Annual utility payments for '68-'72 and '77-'87; property tax paid in all years except '78; and for renters, annual rental payments in all years.

Regardless of the household's tenure the survey inquires as to the number of rooms of the structure. In all but 3 waves ('73, '74, '82) the type of dwelling unit is also recorded: Single-family house; duplex; apartment; mobile home or trailer; rowhouse or townhouse; and other. Limited subjective measures of neighborhood and housing quality are also available, but are of limited use because they are only recorded in six of the earliest waves.

Income and Asset Variables

As its name implies, the Panel Study of Income Dynamics has excellent variables describing respondents' income. Types and amounts of income are presented in very detailed categories and are sometimes available at a monthly level. For this study, fairly broad categories of annual income data are considered: Head and wife's total taxable income, and their total transfer income. Within these two categories there are special measures of interest: Asset income and help from relatives respectively. These four categories are distinguished from one another in the belief that they need not have the same effect on housing decisions.

Although close to being complete, the income data is not perfect. Taxable income is available in every year, but transfer income is not included in the first wave. Head's asset income and help from relatives are available only as bracket variables for '68-'75. Wife's asset income is also bracketed over this period, except that it is not recorded in the first two years of the survey.

Data on asset levels are probably the PSID's biggest weakness. Except for one year (1984) data on asset levels are not recorded. Qualitative questions about the households' savings are only asked intermittently in the early waves and not all asset types are included. Thus it is necessary to use asset income to impute households' asset level.

Demographic Variables

The demographic variables contained in the PSID are quite satisfactory. In each year marital status of head is recorded, with potential responses being married or permanently cohabiting, single, widowed, divorced, or separated. Employment status is also available, with responses in this category as follows: Working, temporarily laid off, unemployed, retired, permanently or temporarily disabled, keeping house, student, and other.

A subjective indicator of head's disability is present in all waves but the first. A more complete categorical health variable is also available, but it is only present in the last four years. In each year the head of household is asked how many children are present in the family unit. The total number of children of each individual is only available as a summary variable for current respondents. A bracket variable describing an individual's educational attainment level is also recorded in all years.

SAMPLE SELECTION, IDIOSYNCRASIES, AND SPECIAL PROCEDURES

In this section the procedures used to select a sample of elderly households for analysis are explained. As with all data, this study has a number of peculiarities and idiosyncrasies associated with it. This section will also describe these problems and the procedures used to deal with them.

Sample Selection and Headship Idiosyncrasies
Because this work is concerned with the analysis of housing decisions at the household level, use of the full individual-level panel is inappropriate because many households will contain more than one elderly individual. Because the PSID defines most of its data according to who is defined as the head of household, (For instance, all members of a particular family will have identical values for "age of head" and "taxable income of head"), the head is selected to provide the data that represents the household.

Because housing changes are this work's primary concern, the households' data must be consistent from one year to the next. A problem could arise if the person designated as head is not the same year to year. Fortunately the PSID is very consistent as to whom they define as head over time. Once a respondent is designated head of household they will remain so until they die or become a nonrespondent. The PSID is also rather sexist in headship definition: The male is always designated the head of household unless he is incapable of answering the questions. This occurs in spite of occasional protests by the male's wife (See The PSID User's Guide (1973)).

The PSID is somewhat strange in that it gives headship status to both a husband who is newly deceased or has moved out, *and* the wife who takes over as head in the year immediately after the husband's exit. Given that most of the analyses in this book use two adjacent years to examine housing this could be a source of some confusion. Fortunately the survey also records a "sequence number" which always has a value of one for the current head and higher values for family members who have moved out or are newly deceased. Selecting respondents based on their sequence number in the second of the two adjacent years then eliminates the possibility that the same household will be measured twice in the sample.

Households in which a wife takes over as head due to the husband's death are of some concern. Housing changes may be more likely to occur in these circumstances as a result of the change in family composition. If the analysis is limited only to those households with the same head in each year, this sort of household will be excluded and important housing changes may be masked. Wives that take over as heads are therefore purposefully included in most of the empirical analyses in this book.

This inclusion necessitates some data redefinition. Recall that most of the family's data is defined as relating to the head. Thus it would be inappropriate to use "employment status of head" to define the working status of a wife who becomes a head. Fortunately enough "wife" and individual-level variables are present to allow the replacement of the previous head's values with the new head's. The only exception is that wife's disability status is unavailable in '68, '73-'75, '79, and '80. In analyses that include this variable, wives that become heads are excluded.

Housing Status Peculiarities

In the previous section, the variable that records whether the household owns, rents, or has some other living arrangement is described. For most respondents this variable is accurate, but for a small number of the dependent elderly it is not. Specifically, some of the elderly who live dependently with relatives are mistakenly given a relative's housing status. These persons are reclassified using a procedure similar to the one developed by the PSID staff in conjunction with David Ellwood and Thomas Kane (1989): Respondents are classified as "dependent sharers" if they are single, move in with relatives, and their income remains less than half of the total family income for at least three years after the move or until they move out.

Another housing change that is not well-defined by the PSID is movement into a nursing home. The survey contains an indicator of nonresponse due to institutionalization, but this is of little use when classifying current respondents. The PSID has a nursing home indicator for current respondents, but only in the last four waves. To classify nursing home residents in earlier years two procedures are used: (1) If possible, their status is backcoded from the earliest wave that the indicator is present; and (2) With another procedure developed by Ellwood and Kane (1989), if the respondent moves for involuntary reasons into housing that has less than 3 rooms and reports that she neither owns nor rents, she is classified as being in a nursing home.

Weights
In its first year, the PSID oversampled the poor and nonwhites because of interest in the special role they play in income dynamics. It also clustered its sample geographically to reduce collection costs. Therefore the PSID staff provides weights for each individual in each year that can be used to adjust for the oversampling. The weights are proportional to the inverse of the probability of selection from the universe of all households in the 48 contiguous states. Over the years of the study the weights have been adjusted to account for family composition changes and differential nonresponse (See The PSID User Guide (1973) for a thorough discussion).

INITIAL EMPIRICAL RESULTS:
MOBILITY RATES AND TRANSITION MATRICES

In this section some simple evidence describing the housing changes taken by the elderly is presented. It begins with the examination of mobility rates and transition matrices over different housing tenures. Attention is then drawn exclusively to the housing decisions of homeowners

---

Table 3.1

Weighted Annual Mobility Rates
within Age Group and Prior Year's Tenure Status

Age	Owners	Renters	Others
50-54	4.50% (706)	20.66% (484)	32.89% (71)
55-59	5.74% (1699)	17.66% (1012)	18.01% (134)
60-64	4.61% (2656)	14.99% (1267)	27.30% (196)
65-69	3.87% (3098)	13.86% (1217)	22.72% (214)
70-74	3.78% (2530)	10.81% (922)	16.01% (183)
75-79	4.82% (1674)	12.96% (551)	10.21% (134)
80-84	6.00% (901)	9.95% (300)	12.76% (105)
85+	8.36% (453)	13.50% (170)	9.04% (86)
All	4.68% (13717)	13.71% (5923)	17.24% (1123)

Note: Numbers in parentheses represent actual un-weighted numbers in each category.

---

with the presentation of cross-tabulations that focus on income, assets, home equity, housing costs, and a number of demographic characteristics.

Observations are defined using variables from two adjacent years. Sample members must be fifty years of age or older in the initial wave of the survey, and they must be a head or wife in the first of the two adjacent years, and have a sequence number equal to one in the second. Observations are then pooled over the twenty years of the panel, which allows nineteen possible cross sections to be observed and pooled together.

Mobility Rates

Table 3.1 presents weighted mobility rates by age bracket. The sample is divided into 3 groups representing the different tenure classifications in the previous year. It appears that mobility rates differ across previous tenure status, with previous renters and those neither owning nor renting (others) having much larger rates than owners. A chi square test (2 degrees of freedom, 1% level) rejects the hypothesis that the aggregate mobility rates do not differ across previous tenure.

Within the owning group, mobility rates appear to form somewhat of a bowl shape, with the minimum occurring when the respondents are in their early 70's. A chi square test rejects the hypothesis that owners' mobility rates are the same across age brackets (7 degrees of freedom, 1% level). A possible explanation for the U-shaped rates is that owners may make housing adjustments when relatively young in response to job and family changes; and when relatively old in response to deteriorating health.

Transition Matrices

Mere mobility rates reveal little about the destination tenure status of those households that move, and thus obscure valuable information. To remedy this problem transition matrices are presented that specify the proportion of each previous tenure group that switch into each tenure group. Table 3.2 presents the matrix for all movers, while Table 3.3 presents the corresponding matrices for different age groups.

Table 3.2
Weighted Tenure Transition Matrix for All Movers

| | | Latter Tenure | | |
		own	rent	other
Previous Tenure	own	.584 (359)	.288 (188)	.128 (86)
	rent	.181 (127)	.713 (672)	.106 (82)
	other	.286 (48)	.369 (85)	.345 (75)

Note: Numbers in parentheses are unweighted cell counts. They do not yield the percentages due to weighting.

Table 3.2 provides evidence that a modest net movement away from home ownership occurs among the elderly. The movement occurs in spite of the fact that non-owners tend to be more mobile. A chi square test confirms that moves away from home ownership constitute a larger percentage of moves than those into home ownership situations.

To explore this topic further the analogous matrices for each age group are presented in Table 3.3. These matrices indicate that the net movement out of home ownership increases with age. If one concentrates on the rows describing homeowners, it is evident that movement into "other" tenure arrangements generally increases with age. Movement from home ownership to rental units appears to increase after age 59. This loose observation is confirmed by a chi square test involving owners only: The hypothesis that the owners' proportions are the same across age groups is rejected at the 1% percent level (10 degrees of freedom).

Table 3.3
Weighted Transition Matrices within Age Group

	own	rent	other
own	.625 (78)	.326 (43)	.048 (11)
rent	.259 (51)	.690 (210)	.050 (17)
other	.397 (15)	.224 (13)	.379 (20)

Age (50-59)

	own	rent	other
own	.793 (85)	.139 (24)	.068 (8)
rent	.270 (36)	.633 (137)	.097 (12)
other	.249 (8)	.429 (25)	.323 (13)

Age (60-64)

	own	rent	other
own	.659 (74)	.231 (26)	.111 (16)
rent	.221 (23)	.649 (133)	.130 (21)
other	.300 (8)	.346 (18)	.354 (18)

Age (65-69)

	own	rent	other
own	.577 (53)	.320 (32)	.102 (11)
rent	.092 (7)	.802 (87)	.106 (12)
other	.174 (5)	.527 (15)	.300 (11)

Age (70-74)

	own	rent	other
own	.333 (28)	.439 (35)	.228 (20)
rent	.115 (8)	.782 (60)	.103 (8)
other	.508 (8)	.162 (4)	.331 (5)

Age (75-79)

	own	rent	other
own	.471 (41)	.301 (28)	.228 (20)
rent	.030 (2)	.778 (45)	.191 (12)
other	.194 (4)	.425 (10)	.381 (8)

Age (80+)

Note: Numbers in parentheses are unweighted cell counts. They do not yield the proportions due to weighting.

The analogous matrix for all non-movers is presented in Table 3.4. The diagonal elements of this matrix are close to one, but cell by cell t-tests reject the hypothesis that the matrix is the identity matrix. This suggests that housing transitions that do not involve moves should not be ignored.

Table 3.4
Weighted Tenure Transition Matrix for All Non-movers

| | | Latter Tenure | | |
		own	rent	other
Previous Tenure	own	.993 (12985)	.002 (33)	.005 (66)
	rent	.013 (58)	.973 (4921)	.014 (63)
	other	.055 (43)	.075 (60)	.870 (812)

Note: Numbers in parentheses are unweighted cell counts. They do not yield the percentages due to weighting.

INITIAL EMPIRICAL RESULTS: CROSSTABULATIONS

In this section attention is paid exclusively to elderly homeowners and the housing transitions that they undertake. The transitions will fall into six categories representing housing decisions that an elderly homeowner may make:
(1) Move to a home with greater home equity;
(2) stay in the current home with no change in status;
(3) move to a home with less home equity;
(4) move to a rental unit;
(5) acquire a new mortgage; and
(6) move into a dependent living arrangement.

This section will report fairly simple results involving crosstabulations on these groups with regards to home equity, imputed asset level, income, housing costs, and a number of demographic characteristics.

Transition Definitions

Housing changes are defined by examining the difference in housing status in two adjacent years. The household's response about moving (move, not move), tenure status (own, rent, other), mortgage status (none, one, two), and the special definitions described above are used to determine changes in housing status.

The easiest housing transition to define is actually not a transition at all: Staying in one's current home with no change in tenure and mortgage status. If a homeowner reports no change in tenure status, does not move, and is not found to have acquired a mortgage, they are classified in the "Stay" category.

For those homeowners that do move and remain in the same tenure, separate categories are defined for those that increase home equity (Incr) and those that decrease home equity (Decr). Home equity is calculated as the difference between reported home value and remaining mortgage principal. Unfortunately, mortgage information is unavailable in some years, and the analysis must be limited to the periods '69-'72, '76-'81, and '83-'87.

Those homeowners who move into a rental unit are placed in a fourth category (Rent). Also included in this category are a small number of homeowners who do not move but report a change in tenure status to renting, and those who report changing to a living arrangement in which housing is part of their compensation.

It is also possible to distinguish a category for those homeowners who acquire a new mortgage (Mort). This group is defined as those homeowners who do not move and report that they do not have a mortgage in the former year and do have one in the latter. Also included in this category are those reporting the acquisition of a second mortgage in years in which this information is available ('69-'72, '79-'81, and '83-'87). To capture new second mortgages in the unavailable years, and to capture those households who pay off a mortgage and acquire a new one in the same year, this category also includes households that increase their remaining mortgage principal by $20,000 or more (1987 dollars).

In some cases a mortgage may be acquired exclusively for the purposes of home improvement. In these cases the new mortgage may actually *increase* home equity by increasing the home's value by more than the amount of the mortgage. Because actions that reduce home equity are of primary interest here, these cases are treated differently: Only households who are determined to have acquired a new mortgage *and* whose home equity declines are included in the "Mort" category. Those who acquire a new mortgage and increase home equity are included in the "Stay" category.

The final category defined in these analyses is a change to a dependent living arrangement (Dep). Most of this category is composed of those who list "other" as their tenure status and report that their housing is paid for by others in the second of the adjacent years. Also include in this category are the dependent sharers described above, those determined to have moved into a nursing home, and a small number of households who neither own nor rent and list "temporary" or "other" as why they don't own or rent.

Transition Percentages

The weighted owner transition percentages for the total pooled sample are presented in Table 3.5. As one would

---

Table 3.5
Weighted Owner Transition Percentages

Incr	Stay	Decr	Rent	Mort	Dep
1.3%	93.5%	1.5%	1.6%	1.4%	.8%
(95)	(7631)	(122)	(128)	(143)	(69)

Note: Numbers in parentheses are unweighted cell counts. They do not yield the percentages due to weighting.

---

expect, remaining in the same housing situation is by far
the most common alternative chosen. Moving into a rental
unit is the next most common alternative. Among those that
move to other owner-occupied housing, decreasing one's home
equity is slightly more common. Reducing home equity by
acquiring a new mortgage is about as common as becoming a
renter or moving to a home with less home equity. Moving
into a dependent living arrangement is the alternative
chosen the least. The results of Table 3.5 provide some
rough evidence that homeowners may wish to dissave out of
their accumulated home equity. Over 5% of the pooled sample
take some sort of action in adjacent years that reduces home
equity.

Table 3.6
Weighted Owner Transition Percentages within Age Group

Age	Incr	Stay	Decr	Rent	Mort	Dep
50-59	1.2%	92.5%	2.0%	1.6%	2.5%	.2%
	(11)	(1069)	(26)	(20)	(36)	(3)
60-64	1.2%	92.7%	2.3%	1.1%	2.2%	.4%
	(17)	(1417)	(31)	(18)	(40)	(9)
65-69	1.4%	94.0%	1.3%	1.1%	1.6%	.6%
	(25)	(1772)	(23)	(21)	(35)	(12)
70-74	1.3%	95.0%	1.0%	1.4%	.7%	.6%
	(19)	(1549)	(17)	(24)	(18)	(10)
75-79	.7%	93.3%	1.2%	2.4%	.7%	1.8%
	(9)	(1012)	(12)	(26)	(9)	(20)
80+	1.7%	92.1%	1.7%	2.2%	.7%	1.6%
	(14)	(812)	(13)	(19)	(5)	(15)

Note: Numbers in parentheses are unweighted cell counts.
They do not yield the percentages due to weighting.

Crosstabulation by Age Group

As an introduction to the analysis, an age group crosstabulation is presented in Table 3.6. The classification by age will be familiar from the previous section. The numbers in the table represent the percentage of each age group choosing the corresponding housing alternative. A number of generalizations emerge as one examines Table 3.6. It appears as though movements into rental situations generally increase as age increases, while acquisitions of new mortgages basically follow the opposite pattern. Movements into dependent relationships appear to occur in more advanced years, while no strong pattern appears in the increase or decrease categories. A chi square test (25 degrees of freedom) rejects the null hypothesis that the transition rates do not vary across age groups.

Home Equity Crosstabulation

The analysis now turns to crosstabulations that are more relevant to the implications of the mathematical model of chapter 2. Table 3.7 presents weighted owner transition percentages by various brackets of home equity held in the year before the transition. Those in the lowest equity brackets appear to have the highest propensity of increasing their home equity by moving. They also have the highest probability of entering a dependent arrangement. Except within the lowest equity category, there appears to be little relationship between home equity and the propensity to move to a rental unit or acquire a new mortgage. Only the propensity to move to a home of lesser equity seems to increase with home equity, and the relationship is not strong.

These observations provide little support for the results of chapter 2, which predict that housing changes that reduce home equity should occur more often at higher levels of equity. Nonetheless, a chi square test (35 degrees of freedom) rejects the hypothesis that there is no variation across home equity groups at the 1% level. However, much of the variation upon which the hypothesis is rejected comes from categories that, if anything, appear to run counter to the implications of the mathematical model.

Table 3.7
Weighted Owner Transition Percentages
within Home Equity Bracket

Home Equity (000's 87$)	Incr	Stay	Decr	Rent	Mort	Dep
Less Than 10	1.9% (12)	90.1% (694)	1.1% (8)	2.4% (19)	1.9% (13)	2.6% (19)
10 to 20	2.1% (18)	93.2% (936)	.8% (12)	1.1% (14)	1.3% (19)	1.4% (11)
20 to 30	1.1% (11)	93.4% (1073)	1.3% (15)	2.1% (20)	1.3% (23)	.8% (6)
30 to 40	1.3% (13)	93.9% (1019)	1.7% (18)	1.2% (15)	1.4% (18)	.6% (8)
40 to 50	.9% (7)	93.9% (857)	1.9% (17)	1.9% (18)	1.2% (19)	.2% (2)
50 to 75	1.2% (19)	93.9% (1564)	1.2% (19)	1.4% (22)	1.4% (26)	1.0% (17)
75 to 100	1.3% (10)	94.1% (779)	1.6% (13)	1.2% (10)	1.1% (13)	.6% (5)
More Than 100	.7% (5)	93.5% (709)	2.8% (20)	1.5% (10)	1.4% (12)	.1% (1)

Note: Numbers in parentheses are unweighted cell counts.
They do not yield the percentages due to weighting.

Imputed Asset Crosstabulation
   Another factor of great interest in this study is the
effect of financial assets on homeowners' propensities to
make various housing changes. As mentioned earlier, the PSID
lacks asset data in almost all of its waves. It does record

income from assets, and therefore this variable is used to impute asset amounts for each household in each wave.

The imputation procedure is as follows: To avoid simultaneity bias, asset income from the year prior to the potential housing change is used. It is assumed that all households hold $200 in non-interest bearing accounts. It is also assumed that the first $100 of interest income comes from assets earning 5% interest. Any amount above that is assumed to accrues from assets earning 10% interest. This

Table 3.8
Weighted Owner Transition Percentages
within Imputed Financial Asset Bracket

Assets (000's 87$)	Incr	Stay	Decr	Rent	Mort	Dep
Less Than 1	.8% (24)	92.5% (3094)	1.4% (47)	2.0% (62)	2.0% (88)	1.4% (43)
1 to 10	1.0% (14)	94.2% (1251)	1.5% (19)	1.6% (22)	.7% (11)	.9% (10)
10 to 30	1.0% (11)	93.7% (1030)	1.6% (17)	1.9% (19)	1.0% (13)	.7% (7)
30 to 50	1.6% (10)	93.7% (609)	1.7% (10)	0.9% (8)	1.3% (9)	.7% (5)
50 to 100	2.6% (22)	93.4% (763)	1.7% (15)	1.2% (10)	1.1% (9)	0% (0)
100 to 200	1.2% (6)	94.3% (522)	2.0% (11)	.5% (3)	1.6% (8)	.4% (2)
More Than 200	2.3% (8)	94.3% (328)	.7% (3)	1.3% (4)	.8% (3)	.6% (2)

Note: Numbers in parentheses are unweighted cell counts. They do not yield the percentages due to weighting.

procedure is admittedly crude, and alternative imputation methods will be explored in the next chapter.

Table 3.8 presents the transition percentages associated with each class of imputed assets. Few clear patterns are evident from an examination of Table 3.8. Those homeowners with high levels of assets seem generally more likely to increase their home equity. A clear relationship is not evident among those that decrease equity, but moving to a rental unit or dependent arrangement seems to be inhibited by greater amounts of assets. The relationship between asset levels and mortgage acquisition is too weak to lead to any conclusions. Despite these weak results, a chi square test with 30 degrees of freedom rejects the hypothesis that there is no variation in housing changes among the asset groups.

Even though the results of these tables are not favorable to the theory put forth in the last chapter, it should not be rejected it yet. There are a number of reasons to believe that the results of these tables are misleading. One is that home equity and financial assets may be highly correlated and simple single dimension crosstabulations may not detect the true underlying relationships. Home equity is also likely to be correlated with the size of the home and the length of tenure in the home, both of which may work counter to the effects of home equity. Another explanation for the mediocre results of the asset analysis is that the imputation procedure may be too imprecise. Perhaps use of an imputation technique using data in the one year in which asset data is available will be more fruitful.

Income Crosstabulation

The effect of income on the housing choices of elderly homeowners is also of some concern. As a first pass at describing this aspect, total taxable and transfer income of the head and wife are combined into a single summary measure of income.

Table 3.9 presents crosstabulations across income groups. By examining Table 3.9 it appears as though income may have a stimulative effect on homeowners' propensity to increase their equity by moving. No distinct pattern occurs within the decrease and new mortgage columns, but greater amounts of income appear to have an inhibiting effect on

Table 3.9
Weighted Owner Transition Percentages
within Total Income Bracket

Income (000's 87$)	Incr	Stay	Decr	Rent	Mort	Dep
Less Than 5	.6% (4)	91.8% (875)	.6% (7)	3.0% (27)	1.8% (19)	2.3% (22)
5 to 10	1.1% (18)	92.9% (1719)	1.4% (22)	1.9% (33)	1.2% (37)	1.5% (28)
10 to 15	1.1% (13)	93.2% (1338)	1.9% (27)	1.8% (23)	1.2% (25)	.9% (10)
15 to 20	1.0% (10)	95.2% (950)	1.2% (12)	1.0% (12)	1.1% (14)	.6% (4)
20 to 30	1.1% (15)	94.4% (1220)	2.0% (26)	1.1% (14)	1.3% (18)	.2% (2)
30 to 50	1.9% (19)	94.2% (984)	1.3% (13)	1.2% (12)	1.5% (17)	0% (0)
More Than 50	2.4% (16)	91.7% (545)	2.4% (15)	1.1% (7)	1.8% (13)	.5% (3)

Note: Numbers in parentheses are unweighted cell counts. They do not yield the percentages due to weighting.

moving into a rental unit and living dependently. A chi square test strongly rejects the hypothesis that there is no difference in change of housing status across income groups. These latter results are largely consistent with the predictions of the mathematical model of chapter 2, which predict income to have an inhibiting effect on home equity reduction.

Housing Cost Crosstabulation
   The final financial variable that is explored in this chapter is a measure of housing costs. This measure is constructed by adding the homeowner's mortgage payment, utility payment, and property tax. In one of the relevant years utility figures are not recorded and in another property tax is not recorded. This reduces the usable sample size by about 20% All figures are annual and come from the wave before the potential housing change. Table 3.10 presents the crosstabulation results.

Table 3.10
Weighted Owner Transition Percentages
within Housing Cost Bracket

Cost (000's 87$)	Incr	Stay	Decr	Rent	Mort	Dep
Less Than 1	1.7% (14)	91.3% (813)	2.0% (15)	.9% (10)	1.7% (22)	2.3% (21)
1 to 2	1.0% (23)	94.0% (2269)	1.5% (40)	1.4% (33)	1.5% (47)	.6% (17)
2 to 3	.6% (7)	94.5% (1294)	1.3% (16)	1.8% (24)	1.3% (20)	.5% (7)
3 to 5	.7% (8)	93.9% (1051)	2.0% (22)	1.9% (22)	1.0% (14)	.5% (5)
More Than 5	2.7% (18)	91.0% (724)	2.2% (17)	1.4% (10)	2.3% (22)	.4% (4)

Note: Numbers in parentheses are unweighted cell counts. They do not yield the percentages due to weighting.

   The results in Table 3.10 are somewhat curious. For most of the housing alternatives, the transition rates are highest at both ends of the housing cost spectrum. The only alternative that appears to follow the predictions of the mathematical model is the rental alternative, with this choice generally becoming more likely as housing costs increase. Nonetheless, and largely because of the values in the high and low brackets, a chi square test (20 degrees of freedom, 1% level), performed on this table rejects the hypothesis that the choice of housing alternative does not vary across the brackets.

Employment Status Crosstabulation
Several non-financial factors are also examined. The first is change in employment status. In Table 3.11 households are classified into four rather coarse groups that describe the head of household's work status before and after the potential move. A number of interesting observations are evident in Table 3.11. Households who stay employed are the least likely to make any housing change, with the exception of the acquisition of a mortgage, which

Table 3.11
Weighted Owner Transition Percentages
within Changes in Employment Status

Employment Change	Incr	Stay	Decr	Rent	Mort	Dep
Remains Working	1.0% (22)	94.5% (1985)	1.3% (29)	.9% (21)	2.4% (58)	.0% (1)
Becomes Working	2.6% (5)	89.9% (192)	3.0% (6)	2.1% (4)	1.5% (3)	.9% (2)
Becomes Non-Working	1.8% (7)	90.7% (431)	2.1% (9)	2.6% (11)	1.6% (9)	1.3% (5)
Remains Non-Working	1.3% (61)	93.5% (5012)	1.5% (77)	1.7% (91)	1.0% (71)	1.1% (60)

Note: Numbers in parentheses are unweighted cell counts. They do not yield the percentages due to weighting.

they are the most likely to do. Exiting the labor force seems to be mildly associated with moves that reduce home equity. Getting a new job is most strongly associated with movements into other owner-occupied homes, although an increase or decrease in home equity appears to be equally likely under these circumstances.

The small numbers of persons experiencing employment changes makes the use of the chi square statistic unadvisable, some of the categories were combined. This would make the result difficult to interpret, so a chi square test performed on the data in Table 3.11.

Disability Status Crosstabulation

A demographic characteristic that may play a large role in the elderly's housing decision is that of health status. The PSID lacks extensive measures of health, and so this analysis relies on a subjective dummy variable describing disability status. Categories are constructed along the

Table 3.12
Weighted Owner Transition Percentages
within Changes in Disability Status

Disability Change	Incr	Stay	Decr	Rent	Mort	Dep
Remains Well	1.3% (47)	94.5% (3482)	1.4% (58)	1.2% (45)	1.3% (64)	.3% (9)
Becomes Well	1.7% (11)	92.1% (702)	2.5% (16)	1.5% (11)	1.5% (15)	.7% (5)
Remains Limited	1.2% (27)	92.0% (2461)	1.4% (33)	2.3% (59)	1.4% (49)	1.7% (44)
Becomes Limited	1.2% (9)	94.2% (877)	1.5% (14)	.8% (10)	1.3% (15)	1.1% (11)

Note: Numbers in parentheses are unweighted cell counts. They do not yield the percentages due to weighting.

lines of the previous subsection, and the results are presented in Table 3.12. The results are consistent with what might be expected. Homeowners that remain or become healthy are more likely to increase home equity than their sickly counterparts. Becoming well also appears to stimulate movement into owner-occupied homes of lesser equity. Remaining disabled is associated with moves into rental units, but becoming disabled seems to inhibit the act of becoming a renter. No strong relationship between disability and mortgage acquisition is evident, but those remaining or becoming disabled are the most likely to enter a dependent living arrangement. A 1% level chi square test with 15 degrees of freedom rejects the hypothesis that those in each type of disability transition come from the same population.

Marital Status Crosstabulation
    The next demographic characteristic considered is that of marital status. Households are categorized as married or

Table 3.13
Weighted Owner Transition Percentages
within Changes in Marital Status

Marital Change	Incr	Stay	Decr	Rent	Mort	Dep
Remains Married	1.5% (63)	94.4% (4262)	1.6% (72)	.8% (36)	1.4% (82)	.3% (12)
Becomes Married	5.2% (1)	76.5% (18)	18.2% (4)	0% (0)	.2% (1)	0% (0)
Remains Unmarried	.9% (28)	92.9% (3169)	1.1% (37)	2.4% (82)	1.3% (54)	1.4% (50)
Becomes Unmarried	1.5% (3)	83.3% (182)	5.1% (9)	4.3% (10)	2.2% (6)	3.5% (7)

Note: Numbers in parentheses are unweighted cell counts. They do not yield the percentages due to weighting.

unmarried in the years before and after a potential move, resulting in a total of four categories. Note that all types of unmarried people are combined: Single, divorced, separated, widowed. Table 3.13 presents the weighted housing transition percentages for each of these groups.

The results of the table suggest that marital status plays a significant role in home ownership decisions. Remaining married seems to have a stabilizing effect on a household's housing arrangements, and particularly seems to inhibit moves into rental units and dependency. Becoming married is associated with moves into other owner-occupied arrangements, although the numbers are too small in this category to lead to strong conclusions. Remaining unmarried seems to encourage moves into rental units and dependency. Becoming unmarried is strongly associated with all types of housing changes, but especially ones that reduce home equity. Again the numbers in some categories are very small, and the chi square test is not performed.

Children Crosstabulation

The final demographic characteristic deals with the effect of children on a homeowner's housing decision. This factor is measured according to the presence of children in the household and any change in their number. Those households that experience no change in the number of children are divided into those that have children (present), and those that don't (not present). Households that do have a change of one or more children are separated into those that experience a decrease in the number of children and those that experience an increase. The results are presented in Table 3.14.

Those that have children and experience no change in the number of children tend to be less likely to increase home equity, and more likely to acquire a new mortgage. In those households where the number of children decreases, moves to homes having less equity, rental units, and the acquisition of a new mortgage are more common. This suggests that a somewhat strong "empty nest" effect is present. Those households that experience an increase in the number of children tend to move to lower equity homes and acquire new mortgages more often. Although these results are suggestive,

Table 3.14
Weighted Owner Transition Percentages
within Changes in Number of Children

Number of Children	Incr	Stay	Decr	Rent	Mort	Dep
No Change (not present)	1.3% (88)	93.6% (6547)	1.5% (100)	1.6% (110)	1.2% (94)	.8% (61)
No Change (present)	.6% (5)	94.0% (712)	1.3% (12)	1.0% (8)	2.7% (24)	.4% (2)
Decrease	.2% (1)	90.7% (290)	2.9% (7)	2.5% (10)	3.0% (17)	.8% (3)
Increase	1.5% (1)	84.0% (82)	3.9% (3)	0% (0)	6.5% (8)	4.1% (3)

Note: Numbers in parentheses are unweighted cell counts.
They do not yield the percentages due to weighting.

the small numbers in some categories again makes a rigorous statistical test impossible.

DISCUSSION AND SUMMARY

Consistent Statistical Significance of Results

The reader should not view the unanimous rejection of null hypotheses as strong evidence as to the validity of the theory presented in chapter 2. The null hypotheses put forth in this chapter are that there is no relationship between a particular variable and housing changes. Thus even relationships that run counter to those hypothesized contribute to the rejection of the null.

One should also be aware that the sample size examined in this chapter is relatively large. The large sample tends to cause statistical significance more frequently than with samples of smaller size. Therefore there may be a very weak and economically insignificant relationship to be statistically significant.

A final reason for viewing the test statistics suspiciously is that the data come from pooled cross sections. Since a single household may contribute multiple observations, the sample could be viewed as not being independent. If households behave similarly year to year they may reduce the variation observed in the sample and increase the size of any test statistic.

Correlation Among Factors

As previously mentioned, many of the variables examined here are likely to be correlated with one another. This is especially true among the variables that perform the worst in this chapter, the financial ones. The correlation, if present, may obscure underlying relationships in some cases and lead to misleading results in others. Rather than attempting to control for the correlation within the context of crosstabulations, multivariate regressions are utilized in the next chapter.

Summary of Results

The crude results of this chapter suggest that demographic considerations may be more important than financial considerations to elderly homeowners' housing decisions. Crosstabulations on marital, employment, and disability status yield strong, intuitively consistent results as to their effect on housing changes. Financial variables, on the other hand, have less consistent results. Home equity and housing costs do not have consistently strong relationships across housing transitions. Where they do have relationships, they are often the opposite from what is indicated by theory. The results for income and asset level are somewhat better, but are not particularly strong.

While these results are suggestive, they still do not provide convincing evidence that demographic factors are dominant, or that financial factors are irrelevant. To gain better insight on these questions multivariate analyses are needed, and are thus taken up in the next chapter.

IV. BINOMIAL PROBIT AND MULTINOMIAL LOGIT ANALYSES

In chapter 3 simple crosstabulations were presented that describe the relationships between a number of variables and the housing decisions of older homeowners. This chapter extends the empirical analysis by using multivariate limited-dependent variable regression techniques to improve our understanding of the elderly's underlying home ownership decision.

The results of this chapter indicate that demographic variables are generally more important than financial variables in explaining elderly homeowners' housing decisions. Coefficients on several demographic variables are consistently found to be statistically significant and large. Coefficients on financial variables are usually found to be small relative to demographic ones, and their statistical significance is not robust across the different models.

BINOMIAL PROBIT ANALYSIS

In this section the more simple of the econometric models is examined: The binomial probit. This section describes the model and discusses the appropriateness of its use in this context. Empirical results are then presented for a number of specifications. The results provide some evidence that financial variables are important to the elderly's home equity decision, but provide stronger evidence that demographic considerations dominate the decision.

The Binomial Probit Model

The solutions to many microeconomic problems are described as the optimal choice of a continuous variable. Profit-maximizing output and utility-maximizing consumption are common examples. Ordinary least squares is most often an appropriate estimation technique to use in these contexts. However many economic decisions are yes/no propositions: They require a decision maker to take a discrete action rather than choose a value on a continuum. In these contexts ordinary least squares is not appropriate, and limited-dependent variable regression techniques must be used. Because housing changes are made infrequently and dramatic changes are often observed, the analyses must be of the latter type. The first limited-dependent technique to be utilized is the binomial probit.

The analysis begins with a relationship represented by the following equation (Maddala, (1983)):

$$(4.1) \qquad y_i^* = \beta'X_i + e_i \qquad i = 1,..,N$$

where y_i^* is an underlying response variable for individual i; β is the coefficient vector of interest; X_i is a vector of independent variables; and e_i is an error term. It is not possible to observe y_i^* directly. Instead,

$$(4.2) \qquad \begin{aligned} y_i &= 1 \qquad \text{if } y_i^* > 0 \\ y_i &= 0 \qquad \text{otherwise.} \end{aligned}$$

Because y_i^* is not observed, it is impossible to perform the conventional least squares technique to estimate β. Instead, the following probabilities are defined:

$$(4.3) \quad \begin{aligned} \text{Prob}(y_i=1) &= \text{Prob}(y_i^* > 0) = \text{Prob}(\beta'X_i + e_i > 0) \\ &= \text{Prob}(e_i > -\beta'X_i) = 1 - F(-\beta'X_i) \\ \text{Prob}(y_i=0) &= \text{Prob}(y_i^* \leq 0) = \text{Prob}(\beta'X_i + e_i \leq 0) \\ &= \text{Prob}(e_i \leq -\beta'X_i) = F(-\beta'X_i) \end{aligned}$$

where $F(\cdot)$ is a cumulative distribution function. Using these probabilities the following likelihood function can be written:

$$(4.4) \qquad L = \prod_{y=0}^{N} F(-\beta'X_i) \prod_{y=1}^{N} [1 - F(-\beta'X_i)]$$

By assuming that $F(\cdot)$ is the cumulative standard normal distribution function and taking logs of equation (4.4), the log likelihood function for the binomial probit model is derived:

(4.5) log(L) =
$$\sum_{i=1}^{N} y_i \cdot \log[\Phi(-\beta'X_i)] + \sum_{i=1}^{N} (1-y_i) \cdot \log[1-\Phi(-\beta'X_i)]$$

The β vector that maximizes equation (4.5) contains the coefficients of interest. There is no closed-form solution for this estimate, but it can be found using iterative procedures.

Table 4.1 - Descriptive Statistics

Variable	Mean	Std. Dev.
Whether Mortgage	0.260	0.439
Mortgage Payment ($1,000's)	0.804	1.79
Property Tax ($1,000's)	0.678	0.735
Utilities ($1,000's)	1.23	0.723
Rooms	5.49	1.43
DU Type	0.855	0.353
Yrs in Home	18.7	12.4
Home Equity ($1,000's)	50.6	42.3
Imputed Assets ($1,000's)	45.1	206.
Taxable Income ($1,000's)	10.3	23.0
Transfer Income ($1,000's)	6.99	7.18
Age (years)	68.5	8.61
Female	0.355	0.479
College	0.0916	0.288
Retired	0.544	0.498
Become Retired	0.0498	0.218
Married	0.583	0.493
Become Widowed	0.0175	0.131
Limited	0.426	0.495
Become Limited	0.109	0.312
Whether Kids	0.141	0.348
Kids Leave	0.0389	0.193
Rels Help	0.0288	0.167
Amt Rels Help ($1,000's)	0.0383	0.341

Application of the Binomial Probit Model

For the purposes of this work, the dichotomous dependent variable of the probit model is defined according to whether the elderly homeowner reduces home equity or not. Specifically, a homeowner is coded 1 if she takes an action that reduces home equity, and 0 if she does not. The data are grouped in this way because the comparative statics of chapter 2 predict that most variables will have similar effects on all types of home equity reduction.

The explanatory variables used in this analysis include all of the factors examined in chapter 3, some at a less aggregated level. Also included are a number of additional factors not examined in chapter 3. The variables can be grouped into four general headings: Housing costs, housing characteristics, financial, and demographic. Complete descriptions of the variables can be found in Appendix A of this chapter. Descriptive statistics for each variable can be found in Table 4.1.

Binomial Probit Results: Initial Specification

For the first probit analysis, the dependent variable is defined as a 1 if the homeowner decreases home equity by moving to another owner-occupied home, changes to a rental unit, enters a dependent housing arrangement or reduces home equity by acquiring a new mortgage. The household is coded 0 if it stays in its current living situation or increases equity by moving.

The results shown in Table 4.2 are for the full pooled cross-sectional sample. Excluding those years with insufficient data and observations with missing values leaves a sample of 6400. Of these, 6.0% are determined to have reduced their home equity.

The most striking results of this regression have to do with demographic characteristics. Coefficients on retirement, marital, and health status are all quite large and most are statistically significant. Being or becoming retired are both positively correlated with equity-reducing moves. Being married seems to inhibit such a move, and losing a spouse greatly increases a homeowner's propensity to reduce home equity. Physical limitation is positively correlated with equity reductions, as is becoming limited,

Table 4.2 - Binary Probit Results
(dependent variable = 1 if reduce equity)

Variable	Coefficient	t-statistic
Constant	-0.849**	-2.923
Whether Mortgage	-0.270**	-2.939
Mortgage Payment	0.0446**	2.068
Property Tax	-0.00764	-0.159
Utilities	0.0124	0.326
Rooms	-0.00357	-0.176
DU Type	-0.135*	-1.886
Yrs in Home	-0.0106**	-4.608
Home Equity	9.40 E-4	1.208
Assets	-0.00128**	-2.753
Taxable Income	8.76 E-4	0.462
Transfer Income	-0.00397	-0.781
Age	-0.00702*	-1.829
Female	0.0723	0.770
College	-0.108	-1.054
Retired	0.144**	2.077
Become Retired	0.279**	2.468
Married	-0.178*	-1.885
Become Widowed	0.558**	3.409
Limited	0.175**	2.958
Become Limited	0.0700	0.786
Whether Kids	0.00762	0.085
Kids Leave	0.288**	2.142
Rels Help	0.0127	0.065
Amt. Rels Help	-0.00897	-0.093

**significant at the 5% level
*significant at the 10% level
# of observations = 6400
- log likelihood = 1406.577

although not significantly. This may be an indication that prolonged disabilities do precipitate a move, while temporary ones do not. Having children present in the home appears to have little effect on home equity reduction, while children leaving is positively related with such a move. Such evidence indicates the presence of an "emptying nest" effect. Age appears to have a negative effect on the desire to reduce home equity. Other demographic variables do not enter significantly.

The variables that measure characteristics of the home generally perform as expected: Years in Home and DU Type both have negative coefficients that are statistically significant. The negative coefficient for length may indicate that homeowners become emotionally attached to their homes as they live there longer, or it may be measuring households' tastes for moving, the so-called mover-stayer effect. The negative parameter estimate for DU Type may indicate that homeowners become more attached to single-family non-mobile homes than they do to duplexes, townhouses or mobile homes. The coefficient on the number of rooms in the original housing arrangement does not enter significantly.

The performance of the financial variables in this regression is mixed. The parameter estimate on asset level is negative and statistically significant, implying that high levels of financial wealth reduce the homeowners' need to draw on home equity. The coefficient on home equity is positive, (as predicted by the theory of chapter 2), but it is not statistically significant. The results for income measures are even less consistent with theory, which predicts that higher levels of income should lessen the propensity to reduce one's home equity. The coefficient on transfer income is indeed negative, (the expected sign), but is not statistically significant. Taxable income's coefficient is actually positive, (and insignificant), the opposite sign from what one would expect.

One explanation for the income variables' poor performance is that high income may allow homeowners to overcome the monetary costs of moving, thus encouraging movement from a home. This may offset income's predicted deterrent effect on any reduction in home equity.

The coefficients pertaining to housing costs also contain mixed results. Having a mortgage on the home appears to deter any reduction in home equity, but having a large mortgage payment encourages such moves. Both of the variables have statistically significant coefficients. The coefficients for property tax and utility payments do not enter with statistical significance.

Binomial Probit Results: Alternative Specifications
One could criticize the preceding specification because it is not clear that all of the observations treated as reducing home equity should be treated as such. For in-

Table 4.3 - Binary Probit Results
(dependent variable = 1 if reduce equity, w/o new mortgage)

Variable	Coefficient	t-statistic
Constant	-1.60**	-4.945
Whether Mortgage	-0.119	-1.155
Mortgage Payment	0.0271	1.092
Property Tax	-0.0273	-0.506
Utilities	0.00133	0.031
Rooms	0.0116	0.510
DU Type	-0.181**	-2.276
Yrs in Home	-0.00857**	-3.363
Home Equity	0.00173**	2.186
Assets	-0.00151**	-2.791
Taxable Income	0.00179	0.861
Transfer Income	-0.00331	-0.578
Age	7.04 E-4	0.165
Female	0.0250	0.247
College	-0.170	-1.410
Retired	0.181**	2.331
Become Retired	0.334**	2.654
Married	-0.260**	-2.521
Become Widowed	0.589**	3.267
Limited	0.144**	2.155
Become Limited	0.0444	0.441
Whether Kids	-0.208*	-1.766
Kids Leave	0.320*	1.854
Rels Help	0.00847	0.038
Amt. Rels Help	-0.0230	-0.190

**significant at the 5% level
*significant at the 10% level
# of observations = 6400
- log likelihood = 1060.262

stance, the acquisition of a new mortgage, while reducing home equity initially, is also a commitment to gradually increase home equity in the future. This is somewhat at odds with their inclusion in a group that supposedly desires to reduce home equity. Also, movers that reduce home equity only slightly by moving to another home may be incorrectly grouped with those that reduce their home equity dramatically. After all, the elderly also move for reasons other than equity reduction, and if they happen to reduce their equity slightly when moving, they should hardly be included with those that undertake meaningful reductions. This section presents the binomial probit results that occur when these groups are treated as not decreasing their home equity.

In the first alternative specification all of those that acquire new mortgages are reclassified into the group that does not reduce equity. The sample size remains 6400, but the percentage of those with their dependent variable equal to 1 is reduced to 4.1%. The results are presented in Table 4.3.

A number of differences between Tables 4.2 and 4.3 are worth mentioning. First, the coefficients on having a mortgage and mortgage payment have become smaller and have lost their statistical significance. This suggests that mortgage considerations play a large role in the decision to acquire a new mortgage, but not in other types of equity-reducing moves. More significantly, the coefficient for home equity has become statistically significant at the 5% level. This difference suggests that the amount of home equity held does not affect the desire to acquire a new mortgage the same way that it affects other equity-reducing housing changes.

Next, those determined not to have reduced their home equity by a large enough amount to merit inclusion in the equity reduction category are reclassified. Those homeowners that move into another owner-occupied home and reduce their home equity by less than 20% have their dependent variable changed to 0. This reduces the percentage of homeowners with dependent variable equal to 1 to 5.4%. The results are reported in Table 4.4.

Table 4.4 - Binary Probit Results
(dependent variable = 1 if reduce equity, 20% or more)

Variable	Coefficient	t-statistic
Constant	-0.825**	-2.730
Whether Mortgage	-0.241**	-2.554
Mortgage Payment	0.0391*	1.749
Property Tax	0.0239	0.495
Utilities	0.0134	0.342
Rooms	-0.00412	-0.197
DU Type	-0.157**	-2.127
Yrs in Home	-0.00813**	-3.417
Home Equity	8.19 E-4	1.010
Assets	-0.00125**	-2.530
Taxable Income	5.66 E-4	0.284
Transfer Income	-0.00815	-1.492
Age	-0.00930**	-2.328
Female	0.126	1.284
College	-0.0510	-0.485
Retired	0.152**	2.136
Become Retired	0.344**	3.024
Married	-0.160	-1.610
Become Widowed	0.572**	3.422
Limited	0.203**	3.306
Become Limited	0.0648	0.695
Kids	0.0304	0.331
Kids Leave	0.319**	2.358
Rels Help	0.0581	0.297
Amt. Rels Help	-0.0142	-0.097

**significant at the 5% level
*significant at the 10% level
# of observations = 6400
- log likelihood = 1295.941

The most significant change between Tables 4.4 and 4.2 has to do with the income variables. The coefficient on taxable income is still the unexpected sign, although now it is closer to 0. Also the coefficient on transfer income is now much more negative. These changes suggest that income has a stimulative impact on all moves and an inhibiting effect on moves intended to significantly reduce home equity.

Discussion

The results from the binomial probit analyses generally support the theoretic predictions of the second chapter: Housing costs are found to be positively correlated with moves that reduce home equity. In some specifications, the amount of a homeowner's housing equity is found to be positively associated with moves that reduce home equity. Imputed asset levels are found to deter equity-reducing moves. The results for income are less impressive, but evidence suggests that income deters equity reduction while at the same time encouraging mobility.

However, often the coefficients on these economic variables are not statistically significant. Housing costs and income in particular are not consistently significant across specifications. Additionally, the magnitudes of the economic parameter estimates are dwarfed by those for demographic factors. Taking the coefficients of Table 4.3 as an example, it is evident that becoming retired has the same effect on the probability of equity reduction as does having over $193,000 of home equity, everything else held equal. Being married has the same inhibiting effect as having over $172,000 in financial assets or having an extra $78,000 in yearly transfer income. Becoming widowed has the same effect on the probability of equity reduction as $340,000 in home equity; or in the opposite direction, $390,000 in financial assets or over $170,000 of transfer income. These magnitudes indicate that economic forces are relatively weak compared to demographic ones.

Table 4.5 displays changes in the probability of reducing home equity from a one unit change in in each of the dependent variables. The baseline probability is calculated by using the coefficients in Table 4.3, and evaluating all dummy variables at 0, all discrete variables at the nearest integer to their mean, and all continuous variables at their mean (with the exception that mortgage payment and amount of help from relatives are set equal to 0). This procedure yields a baseline probability of .0484. When the

Table 4.5 - Probability Changes
(Changes in probability from a one unit
increase in each independent variable)

Variable	Change in Probability
Whether Mortgage	-.0108
Mortgage Payment	.00227
Property Tax	-.00268
Utilities	.000134
Rooms	.00118
DU Type	-.0156
Yrs in Home	-.000855
Home Equity	.000174
Assets	-.000151
Taxable Income	.000180
Transfer Income	-.000332
Age	.0000708
Female	.00257
College	-.0149
Retired	.0211
Become Retired	.0440
Married	-.0202
Become Widowed	.0642
Limited	.0163
Become Limited	.00464
Kids	-.0175
Kids Leave	.0300
Rels Help	.000858
Amt. Rels Help	-.00230

variable to be analyzed depends on another variable being different from this baseline, (for instance becoming widowed requires that one be married initially), the baseline probability is altered to reflect this.

The figures in Table 4.5 provide further evidence that demographic factors dominate financial ones. Increases in financial variables by $1000 consistently cause changes in predicted probabilities of less than .3%. Changes in demographic variables almost all lead to changes in probability of over 1%, and for certain variables over 4%.

MULTINOMIAL LOGIT ANALYSIS

One could criticize the simple probits of the previous section because the specification of the dependent variable treats all types of home equity reductions similarly. Misleading results could occur if an explanatory variable has an inhibiting effect on one sort of equity reduction and an stimulating effect on another. For instance, becoming physically limited could deter a move to a smaller home but precipitate a move to a dependent living arrangement. The problem is rectified by employing a multinomial logit technique.

The Multinomial Logit Model

The advantage of the multinomial logit model is that one can specify an economic problem as one in which an agent makes a choice among a number of alternatives. This is particularly well-suited to the problem at hand, where an elderly homeowner must choose among a number of housing alternatives.

In general, the explanatory variables of a multinomial logit analysis can include both characteristics of the economic agent and characteristics of the choices she confronts. In the context of housing choice, characteristics of the alternatives are unlikely to be observed, (unless they are chosen) and therefore only household characteristics are included as explanatory variables. The probability of elderly household i choosing living arrangement j can be written as follows (Maddala, (1983)):

$$(4.6) \qquad P_{ij} = \frac{\exp(\beta_j' x_i)}{\displaystyle\sum_{k}^{M} \exp(\beta_k' x_i)} \qquad \begin{aligned} i &= 1,..,N \\ j &= 1,..,M \end{aligned}$$

where N is the number of observations and M is the number of alternatives. Using these probabilities, the log-likelihood function can be written

$$(4.7) \qquad \ln(L) \; = \; \sum_i^M \sum_j^M \; d_{ij} \cdot \ln \left[\frac{\exp(\beta_j' x_i)}{\sum_k^M \exp(\beta_k' x_i)} \right]$$

where d_{ij} is an indicator variable equal to 1 if person i chooses alternative j.

All of the parameters in equation (4.7) are not identified. To estimate the model the β vector must be normalized by setting one alternative's parameters equal to 0. The other parameters are calculated relative to the parameters for the null alternative. The number of parameters to estimate is (M-1) times the number of individual characteristics. The maximization of equation (4.7) has no closed-form solution for β, so an iterative approach must be used.

Model Specification

The multinomial logit model allows the elderly home-owner's housing choices to be specified as a set of several alternatives: Increasing home equity by moving to another owner-occupied unit (increase), staying in the current home (stay), decreasing equity by moving to another owner-occupied unit (decrease), moving into a rental unit (rent), entering a dependent living situation (dependent), and acquiring a new mortgage (mortgage). Note that the terms increase and decrease apply only to those homeowners who change their home equity levels by moving to another owner-occupied home.

An attractive choice for the alternative whose coefficients are zero is the choice to stay in the current home. Thus, coefficients reported for the other alternatives display effects relative to coefficients of the stayers (e.g. $(\beta_{rent}-\beta_{stay})$). This specification fits well with the theoretical analysis of chapter 2, where the gain in utility from housing changes is described relative to no housing change.

Data Restrictions and Enhancements

Unfortunately, it is necessary to impose a number of restrictions on the data in order to estimate the multinomial logit model. Three of the 6400 observations used in the binomial probit analysis are excluded from this analysis because their high levels of imputed assets interfere with the iterative hill-climbing technique used to estimate the model. Of the remaining 6397 observations, 5948 stay in their original home with no housing change, 69 increase home equity by moving to another home, 107 decrease home equity by moving to another home, 95 move to rental units, 57 enter dependent living arrangements, and 121 acquire new mortgages. (Refer to chapter 3 for a complete discussion of category definition.)

The number of observations in some of the categories is relatively small. This is a concern only when all of those choosing one of the alternatives have identical values for explanatory variables. Perfect collinearity is created between the constant and the homogeneous variable within the group, and the parameter estimate for the variable in that group is not estimable. Unfortunately it is necessary to exclude some variables that are included in the probit analysis. The variables affected are: (1) Help from relatives variables - because in the sample no increaser or decreaser receives any monetary help from their relatives; and (2) Whether children left the family unit - because no increaser has children leave. The college dummy variable is also omitted.

A number of variables are also enhanced compared to their use in the binomial probit model. Most importantly, more sophisticated techniques are employed to impute the level of financial assets. In the first analysis of this type, assets are imputed by dividing asset income by the rate of return on three-month treasury bills prevailing in the appropriate year. (Other methods are employed below.) Less importantly, mortgage payment and property tax are adjusted to reflect tax deductibility. The households' itemization status and marginal tax rate are determined according to the procedures used in the PSID's 1979 wave. These modifications change the descriptive statistics of the sample slightly, and new descriptive statistics are reported in Table 4.6.

Table 4.6 - Descriptive Statistics
Multinomial Logit Sample

Variable	Mean	Std. Dev.
Whether Mortgage	0.260	0.439
Mortgage Payment ($1,000's)	0.735	1.61
Property Tax ($1,000's)	0.628	0.651
Utilities ($1,000's)	1.23	0.719
Rooms	5.48	1.43
DU Type	0.855	0.353
Yrs in Home	18.7	12.4
Home Equity ($1,000's)	50.5	42.1
Imputed Assets ($1,000's)	55.4	143.
Taxable Income ($1,000's)	10.3	23.0
Transfer Income ($1,000's)	6.99	7.18
Age (years)	68.5	8.60
Female	0.355	0.479
Retired	0.543	0.498
Become Retired	0.0494	0.217
Married	0.583	0.493
Become Widowed	0.0175	0.131
Limited	0.426	0.495
Become Limited	0.109	0.312
Whether Kids	0.142	0.349

Multinomial Logit Results: Initial Specification

In the first specification, a relatively simple model that defines the choice set as containing the six alternatives described above is employed. The results of this initial multinomial logit regression are presented in Table 4.7. The results differ from the binomial probit results in important ways. Demographic effects have a fairly large impact on certain types of moves. Advancing age is significantly and positively correlated with moves into dependency, probably because age captures deteriorating health aspects not captured by the limitation variables. Age is significantly and negatively associated with the acquisition of a new mortgage. This may be due to discrimination on the part of financial institutions, or because the very old may gain little from the funds derived from the mortgage.

Table 4.7 - Initial Multinomial Logit Results
(Part 1 - Increase and Decrease)

Variable	Increase		Decrease	
	Coefficient	t-stat	Coefficient	t-stat
Constant	-3.80**	-5.060	-2.78**	-4.778
Whether Mort	-0.0599	-0.154	-0.111	-0.308
Mort Payment	0.0943	1.194	-0.0116	-0.118
Property Tax	0.342**	2.767	-0.0518	-0.287
Utilities	0.0815	0.475	-0.0284	-0.191
Rooms	0.0127	0.125	0.0164	0.206
DU Type	-0.884**	-3.069	-0.268	-0.994
Yrs in Home	-0.0381**	-3.079	-0.0432**	-4.425
Home Equity	-0.0167**	-3.306	0.00439**	2.509
Assets	9.44 E-4*	1.671	-0.00115	-1.072
Taxable Inc	0.0112**	3.454	8.95 E-4	0.163
Transfer Inc	0.0389**	2.143	-0.003844	-0.225
Age	0.0151	0.802	-0.0213	-1.340
Female	0.0146	0.029	-0.481	-1.341
Retired	-0.00360	-0.010	0.382	1.324
Bec Retired	0.604	1.233	0.287	0.629
Married	0.318	0.662	-0.306	-0.904
Bec Widowed	-0.143	-0.134	0.816	1.304
Limited	-0.0340	-0.122	-7.71 E-4	-0.003
Bec Limited	-0.266	-0.588	0.0776	0.235
Whether Kids	-1.09**	-2.000	-0.0947	-0.313

*significant at the 10% level   # of observations = 6397
**significant at the 5% level   - log likelihood = 2159.09

Table 4.7 - Initial Multinomial Logit Results
(Part 2 - Rent and Dependent)

Variable	Rent Coefficient	t-stat	Dependent Coefficient	t-stat
Constant	-3.58**	-5.878	-6.00**	-6.378
Whether Mort	0.198	0.525	-1.74**	-2.805
Mort Payment	-0.0837	-0.722	0.442**	4.660
Property Tax	0.298**	2.319	-1.116**	-2.505
Utilities	0.0621	0.431	-0.00255	-0.012
Rooms	0.0569	0.698	0.0308	0.280
DU Type	-0.787**	-3.014	0.189	0.444
Yrs in Home	-0.0201**	-2.152	0.00450	0.406
Home Equity	0.00270	0.976	-0.00565	-0.876
Assets	-0.00614**	-2.735	-9.65 E-4	-0.489
Taxable Inc	0.00606	0.775	-0.0312	-1.066
Transfer Inc	-0.0155	-0.708	-0.0453	-1.132
Age	-0.00816	-0.534	0.0409**	2.108
Female	0.116	0.354	0.633	1.356
Retired	0.674**	2.414	0.340	1.024
Bec Retired	1.14**	2.762	1.76**	3.082
Married	-1.02**	-2.851	-0.516	-0.964
Bec Widowed	1.26**	1.962	1.948**	2.875
Limited	0.345	1.455	1.11**	2.855
Bec Limited	-0.294	-0.695	0.887*	1.766
Whether Kids	-0.347	-0.956	-0.528	-0.839

*significant at the 10% level   # of observations = 6397
**significant at the 5% level   - log likelihood = 2159.09

Table 4.7 - Initial Multinomial Logit Results
(Part 3 - Mortgage)

Variable	Mortgage Coefficient	t-stat
Constant	-2.62**	-4.425
Whether Mort	-1.21**	-3.594
Mort Payment	0.155**	2.155
Property Tax	0.0542	0.262
Utilities	0.0949	0.717
Rooms	-0.0762	-0.994
DU Type	0.0178	0.066
Yrs in Home	-0.0315**	-3.514
Home Equity	-0.00384	-1.000
Assets	-8.91 E-4	-0.707
Taxable Inc	6.74 E-4	0.099
Transfer Inc	-0.00108	-0.059
Age	0.0531**	-3.482
Female	0.521	1.323
Retired	0.150	0.579
Bec Retired	0.150	0.337
Married	0.214	0.547
Bec Widowed	0.577	0.977
Limited	0.417*	1.935
Bec Limited	0.273	0.846
Whether Kids	0.690**	2.960

*significant at the 10% level   # of observations = 6397
**significant at the 5% level   - log likelihood = 2159.09

Being and becoming retired is significantly correlated with moves into rental units, and becoming retired is very strongly associated with moves into dependency. The retirement variables' effect on moves to other owner-occupied housing is not statistically significant. These observations suggest that the onset of retirement may be related to an increase in households' preference for rental and alternative housing.

Being married appears to significantly deter moves into rental arrangements, but seems to have statistically insignificant effects on the propensity to make other moves. Becoming widowed is strongly related to moves into rental units and dependency, with the effect being especially large for the dependency alternative. These results suggests that married couples have a strong preference for owner-occupied housing.

Physical limitation and becoming limited appear to have very strong positive effects on movements into dependency. These factors also appear to precipitate the acquisition of a new mortgage. The coefficients for the limitation variables in other groups are relatively small and not statistically significant. A possible explanation for the weak results is that the onset of disability may have countervailing effects: The illness could create large expenses that could precipitate home equity reduction, but it may also deter a sick homeowner from moving out of fear that the added strain of dislocation may worsen the condition.

The presence of children in the household seems to deter increases in home equity. It may be that the added expense of children prevents homeowners from being able to afford a larger home. Having children present in the home also appears to encourage the acquisition of a new mortgage. The added expense of children combined with the desire to not disrupt the children with an equity-reducing move may make acquiring a new mortgage an attractive way to reduce equity.

Housing characteristics appear to play some role in these regressions. Living in a single-family unit (DU Type = 1) seems to inhibit equity increases. This may be the result of those owners living in multiple-unit structures wishing to move to a separate unit, and in the process increase their equity. Living in a single-family unit also seems to discourage movement to a rental unit. This provides further evidence that the elderly have a preference for separate dwellings. The length of tenure variable is negative and statistically significant for all alternatives except dependency. As with the probit results, this may be an indication of attachment to home or it may be measuring a mover-stayer effect.

The results for the financial variables are interesting and are not always consistent with the theory presented in chapter 2. The coefficients on the level of home equity are statistically significant only for the increase and decrease alternatives. High home equity is positively associated with moves that increase home equity. This result is at odds with the theory of chapter 2, but is consistent with the idea that elderly homeowners with large amounts of equity have little desire to increase it. As expected, high levels of home equity are associated with moves to homes with lower equity and moves to rental units, although the effect for renters is not statistically significant. The opposite is true for moves into dependency, where the coefficient is negative and insignificant. This result is interesting, since it suggests that the elderly only wish to reduce home equity while they can still take advantage of the extra consumption it provides, not when they must live dependently.

The results pertaining to asset levels are more consistent with the mathematical model, but are not generally statistically significant. High asset levels seem to deter equity-reducing moves, although statistical significance occurs only for the renting alternative. High levels of financial assets are positively correlated with increases in home equity.

The coefficient values for the income variables are the most disappointing of the financial factors. Both taxable and transfer income enter significantly only for those that increase equity, where they have the expected positive sign. For all of the other alternatives the coefficients on both types of income are relatively small and are not statistically significant.

The various measures of housing cost generally fail to have the predicted effects, and some have the opposite sign from what is expected. The variables describing mortgage status enter the regression significantly only for the dependency and new mortgage groups: Having a mortgage seems to deter these actions, but large mortgage payments appear to encourage them. Property tax payments enter significantly in three of the five alternatives, but only one has the expected sign. As expected, high property tax payments promote moves to rental housing. However, they unexpectedly encourage moves to homes with higher home equity, and curiously seem to deter moves to dependency. Utility payments do not enter significantly in any of the housing alternatives.

Multinomial Logit Results: Alternative Specifications

One could criticize these results on the basis that they may be sensitive to the method of asset imputation. A number of other imputation procedures were explored. One alternative specification did not attempt to impute asset levels and merely included asset income as a regressor. Other specifications explored the sensitivity of the results to using rates of return other than those on three-month treasury bills. Rates from a wide variety of other assets (corporate bonds, treasury bonds, savings deposits) were used. None of these alternatives yielded regression results substantively different from those already reported, so they are not reported.

Those simple imputation methods could be flawed in a number of ways: Households are likely to hold at least some of their financial wealth in a non-income generating form. They are also likely to hold some wealth in conservative, low-interest forms, and the remainder in more risky, high-interest forms. Moreover, the proportion held in each of these forms is likely to depend on whether the head of household is retired or still working, as well as marital status and age. The amounts of assets held are also likely to show a much higher degree of variance than a simple non-stochastic imputation procedure would imply.

To address these concerns a stochastic regression imputation procedure is employed (Little and Rubin, 1987). Data from the one wave of the PSID in which assets are observable (1984) are used. A sample of homeowners over 50 years of age is extracted, and data on total asset level and asset income is recorded. Spline regressions of asset level on asset income (with a kink point at $1000 of asset income), marital status and age are separately estimated for retired and unretired homeowners. The results are presented in Table 4.8. The coefficients generated by these regressions are used in conjunction with the retirement status, asset income, marital status and age of the pooled cross-sectional sample to generate non-stochastic imputed asset levels. Then a normally distributed error term having a standard deviation equal to that of the regressions' residuals is added to derive imputed asset levels.

Table 4.8 - Asset Imputation Regression
Dependent Variable = Assets in 1987$

Variable	Retired Coefficient	t-stat	Not Retired Coefficient	t-stat
Constant	8585.28	0.481	9794.05	0.709
Asset Inc	21.89	1.616	42.29	3.148
Asset Inc-1000	-9.29	-0.665	-29.95	-2.151
Age-50	-649.25	-0.913	-1265.60	-1.581
Married	19233.37	1.532	33472.93	2.585
# of observations	496		613	
R-squared	.412		.281	

The results of the multinomial logit regression with asset levels imputed in this way are presented in Table 4.9. Most coefficients are largely unchanged, the notable exceptions being for the imputed asset variable. The coefficient for the increase alternative is now statistically significant, and the magnitude and significance for the rental alternative becomes much smaller. The results of a regression that used a non-stochastic version of this asset imputation suggest that these differences are due to the stochastic nature of the imputation rather than the spline regression itself.

Table 4.9 - Multinomial Logit Results
with Stochastic Asset Imputation
(Part 1 - Increase and Decrease)

	Increase		Decrease	
Variable	Coefficient	t-stat	Coefficient	t-stat
Constant	-3.85**	-5.111	-2.76**	-4.760
Whether Mort	-0.0469	-0.121	-0.102	-0.281
Mort Payment	0.0895	1.134	-0.0107	-0.109
Property Tax	0.335**	2.732	-0.0630	-0.348
Utilities	0.0852	0.494	-0.0284	-0.191
Rooms	0.0142	0.140	0.0154	0.193
DU Type	-0.861**	-2.981	-0.265	-0.984
Yrs in Home	-0.0380**	-3.063	-0.0426**	-4.383
Home Equity	-0.0173**	-3.417	0.00420**	2.406
Assets	0.00127**	2.364	-5.62 E-4	-0.965
Taxable Inc	0.0105**	3.219	0.00348	0.066
Transfer Inc	0.0378**	2.073	-0.00509	-0.302
Age	0.0156	0.827	-0.0227	-1.434
Female	0.0405	0.079	-0.485	-1.352
Retired	-0.00816	-0.024	0.371	1.291
Bec Retired	0.576	1.174	0.296	0.649
Married	0.331	0.690	-0.295	-0.870
Bec Widowed	-0.167	-0.156	0.821	1.312
Limited	-0.0410	-0.147	-0.00701	-0.031
Bec Limited	-0.258	-0.570	0.0757	0.229
Whether Kids	-1.09**	-2.002	-0.0862	-0.285

*significant at the 10% level   # of observations = 6397
**significant at the 5% level   - log likelihood = 2163.89

Table 4.9 - Multinomial Logit Results
with Stochastic Asset Imputation
(Part 2 - Rent and Dependent)

Variable	Rent Coefficient	t-stat	Dependent Coefficient	t-stat
Constant	-3.57**	-6.013	-6.01**	-6.398
Whether Mort	0.252	0.670	-1.74**	-2.795
Mort Payment	-0.0722	-0.634	0.442**	4.663
Property Tax	0.259*	1.929	-1.13**	-2.536
Utilities	0.0692	0.479	9.98 E-4	0.005
Rooms	0.0481	0.587	0.0302	0.275
DU Type	-0.698**	-2.671	0.201	0.472
Yrs in Home	-0.0179*	-1.837	0.00495	0.448
Home Equity	4.66 E-4	0.149	-0.00607	-0.950
Assets	-2.01 E-4	-0.323	-2.57 E-4	-0.303
Taxable Inc	0.00253	0.423	-0.0312	-1.071
Transfer Inc	-0.0236	-1.104	-0.0466	-1.170
Age	-0.0134	-0.889	0.0403**	2.081
Female	0.0821	0.252	0.633	1.357
Retired	0.648**	2.343	0.339	1.020
Bec Retired	1.13**	2.743	1.74**	3.093
Married	-1.03**	-2.905	-0.509	-0.951
Bec Widowed	1.32**	2.050	1.96**	2.886
Limited	0.381	1.619	1.12**	2.882
Bec Limited	-0.267	-0.635	0.886*	1.765
Whether Kids	-0.268	-0.737	-0.518	-0.824

*significant at the 10% level   # of observations = 6397
**significant at the 5% level   - log likelihood = 2163.89

Table 4.9 - Multinomial Logit Results
with Stochastic Asset Imputation
(Part 3 - Mortgage)

Variable	Mortgage Coefficient	t-stat
Constant	-2.61**	-4.417
Whether Mort	-1.21**	-3.592
Mort Payment	0.157**	2.174
Property Tax	0.0490	0.235
Utilities	0.0950	0.718
Rooms	-0.0761	-0.994
DU Type	0.0185	0.069
Yrs in Home	-0.0312**	-3.490
Home Equity	-0.00405	-1.067
Assets	-4.74 E-4	-0.782
Taxable Inc	3.43 E-4	0.051
Transfer Inc	-0.00180	-0.098
Age	-0.0540**	-3.549
Female	0.520	1.319
Retired	0.145	0.560
Bec Retired	0.154	0.346
Married	0.227	0.579
Bec Widowed	0.585	0.991
Limited	0.420*	1.949
Bec Limited	0.268	0.830
Whether Kids	0.696**	2.992

*significant at the 10% level   # of observations = 6397
**significant at the 5% level   - log likelihood = 2163.89

An Additional Category

For the final alternative specification, the original asset imputation procedure is reinstated, but another alternative category is specified. One could criticize the construction of the increase and decrease categories because they include homeowners who move from one home to another and change their home equity slightly in the process of moving may be included incorrectly with those that increase or decrease their home equity by a large amount.

To address this problem, a new category is formed that contains households that move from one owner-occupied unit to another and change their home equity by less than 20%. This specification takes 24 observations from the original Increase category and 39 observations from the Decrease category and places them in a new category dubbed "Little Change". For the multinomial logit regression of this new specification, it is necessary to eliminate the variable that indicates the onset of widowhood because none of the remaining homeowners who increase home equity become widowed. The results are presented in Table 4.10.

The most striking result in this regression is that the coefficients on both taxable and transfer income are positive and significant for the new category. This suggests that high levels of income enable homeowners to overcome the transaction costs involved in moving to homes with similar levels of equity. It also suggests that for the alternatives in which equity is reduced, the positive effect of income on the ability to overcome transaction costs may counteract the inhibiting effect of high income on the desire to reduce home equity.

Discussion

The results of this section provide some supportive evidence for the theoretic predictions of chapter 2. The amount of home equity is generally positively correlated with homeowners' propensity to reduce equity, and financial assets have a generally negative relationship with equity-reducing moves. However, these effects are not consistent nor statistically significant across all of the equity-reducing alternatives. Even weaker evidence is presented regarding the effects of housing costs and income, although

Table 4.10 - Multinomial Logit Results
with "Little Change" Category
(Part 1 - Increase and Decrease)

Variable	Increase Coefficient	t-stat	Decrease Coefficient	t-stat
Constant	-2.72**	-3.315	-3.366**	-4.453
Whether Mort	-0.189	-0.400	0.446	0.997
Mort Payment	0.123	1.237	-0.153	-1.115
Property Tax	0.294*	1.802	0.180	0.973
Utilities	0.119	0.574	-0.609	-0.323
Rooms	-0.0849	-0.680	0.0437	0.446
DU Type	-0.918**	-2.639	-0.521	-1.576
Yrs in Home	-0.0291**	-1.988	-0.0305**	-2.511
Home Equity	-0.0221**	-2.801	0.00524**	2.792
Assets	0.0142**	2.805	-5.29 E-4	-0.437
Taxable Inc	0.00493	0.579	5.86 E-5	0.009
Transfer Inc	0.0210	0.815	-0.0269	-1.158
Age	-0.00532	-0.229	-0.0559**	-2.632
Female	-0.318	-0.612	-0.0978	-0.200
Retired	0.0721	0.169	0.645*	1.764
Bec Retired	0.493	0.760	0.862*	1.815
Married	-0.172	-0.354	-0.0626	-0.133
Limited	-0.113	-0.337	0.0541	0.190
Bec Limited	-0.567	-0.909	0.00322	0.008
Whether Kids	-1.41*	-1.871	0.0503	0.148

*significant at the 10% level   # of observations = 6397
**significant at the 5% level   - log likelihood = 2220.14

Table 4.10 - Multinomial Logit Results
with "Little Change" Category
(Part 2 - Rent and Dependent)

Variable	Rent Coefficient	t-stat	Dependent Coefficient	t-stat
Constant	-3.67**	-5.971	-6.40**	-6.590
Whether Mort	0.201	0.529	-1.78**	-2.861
Mort Payment	-0.0892	-0.763	0.437**	4.609
Property Tax	0.295**	2.332	-1.06**	-2.407
Utilities	0.0616	0.430	0.00142	0.007
Rooms	0.0561	0.688	0.0251	0.229
DU Type	-0.793**	-3.035	0.153	0.360
Yrs in Home	-0.0203**	-2.178	0.00340	0.307
Home Equity	0.00266	0.969	-0.00621	-0.960
Assets	-0.00621**	-2.760	-0.00106	-0.525
Taxable Inc	0.00584	0.740	-0.0336	-1.147
Transfer Inc	-0.0153	-0.697	-0.0399	-1.025
Age	-0.00706	-0.461	0.0436**	2.249
Female	0.236	0.698	1.09**	2.097
Retired	0.666**	2.391	0.306	0.922
Bec Retired	1.15**	2.772	1.78**	3.171
Married	-0.852**	-2.375	0.126	0.235
Limited	0.346	1.460	1.11**	2.853
Bec Limited	-0.274	-0.649	0.915*	1.830
Whether Kids	-0.341	-0.939	-0.528	-0.839

*significant at the 10% level   # of observations = 6397
**significant at the 5% level   - log likelihood = 2220.14

Table 4.10 - Multinomial Logit Results
with "Little Change" Category
(Part 3 - Mortgage and Little Change)

Variable	Mortgage Coefficient	t-stat	Little Change Coefficient	t-stat
Constant	-2.73**	-4.627	-4.84**	-5.990
Whether Mort	-1.21**	-3.599	-0.614	-1.315
Mort Payment	0.155**	2.142	0.129	1.367
Property Tax	0.0552	0.271	0.0194	0.088
Utilities	0.0942	0.713	0.0275	0.147
Rooms	-0.0777	-1.015	0.0535	0.502
DU Type	0.0130	0.048	-0.168	-0.487
Yrs in Home	-0.0316**	-3.518	-0.0630**	-4.613
Home Equity	-0.00384	-1.006	-0.0493	-1.033
Assets	-9.15 E-4	-0.725	-0.0193	-1.558
Taxable Inc	6.12 E-4	0.090	0.0127**	3.003
Transfer Inc	-5.55 E-4	-0.030	0.0501**	2.646
Age	-0.0525**	-3.442	0.0483**	2.462
Female	0.659*	1.726	-0.355	-0.706
Retired	0.142	0.548	-0.059	-0.158
Bec Retired	0.152	0.342	-0.334	-0.479
Married	0.357	0.952	0.184	0.398
Limited	0.414*	0.975	-0.0623	-0.210
Bec Limited	0.278	0.861	0.151	0.365
Whether Kids	0.694**	2.979	-0.690	-1.263

*significant at the 10% level   # of observations = 6397
**significant at the 5% level   - log likelihood = 2220.14

there is some reason to believe that income encourages mobility while simultaneously reducing the desire to reduce home equity.

The results for demographic variables are stronger than those for the financial variables. The onset of retirement has a statistically significant and strongly positive relationship with moves where home equity is reduced and the household remains independent. Being married strongly inhibits moves out of home ownership, and becoming widowed seems to precipitate such moves. Physical disability is strongly correlated with moves into dependent living arrangements. As with the binomial probit analyses, the magnitudes of the demographic coefficients are much larger than their financial counterparts.

If one examines the coefficient values across moves that reduce home equity, (decrease, rent, dependent, new mortgage), one easily recognizes that the values are very dissimilar. In some cases there are coefficients on the same variable that have opposite signs, and sometimes both are statistically significant. The observation suggests that the multinomial logit specification is more appropriate than the binomial probit, where the dissimilar alternatives are combined.

CRITICISMS

Despite the large number of specifications presented above, a number of criticisms remain. Three of the most important are addressed in this section.

Use of Pooled Data

One could criticize both the probit and logit regressions because they make use of pooled cross-sectional data. Under these conditions, some households contribute more than one observation to the total sample. If unobserved individual-specific effects are present, they may create a lower degree of variance in the sample than if each individual contributed one observation. Thus the t-statistics reported for the regressions may be unfairly high.

Joint Decisions

Another potential criticism of the regressions is that they utilize several explanatory variables that are better thought of as joint choice variables. For example, elderly homeowners probably make *joint* decisions regarding retirement and housing, rather than deciding each issue separately. Furthermore, asset levels are more appropriately viewed as endogenous (even though they are measured in the year prior to the potential housing change) because they are likely to have been chosen as part of a multi-year optimization plan. (Indeed, the mathematical model of chapter 2 suggests that this is the case.) This is particularly troubling in that demographic variables may be affecting housing changes via their effect on long-term retirement and asset decisions. This may tend to confuse the separation of financial and demographic effects. Ideally, one would like to capture the interdependent aspects of the joint choice of housing, retirement and asset levels. While conceptually it is possible to address this issue with a simultaneous equation procedure or a joint decision model, the imperfect data on asset levels and the low incidence of housing and retirement changes make such an approach infeasible with the data described here.

Forward-Looking Considerations

A related criticism of the results involves the forward-looking nature of the housing decision. Elderly homeowners' decisions regarding housing not only depend of current income, assets and home equity, but also on the homeowners' expectations of what these variables will be in the future. Demographic variables such as retirement, marital and limitation status may act as signals for expected changes in income, assets and other financial factors. If so, the demographic variables' magnitude and significance may not be due to their direct role in the housing decision, but rather to the fact that they signal future changes in financial considerations.

SUMMARY AND DISCUSSION

The preceding sections have provided a good deal of evidence concerning the housing decisions of elderly homeowners. Most of the results are consistent with the theoretic framework of chapter 2. The results also suggest that demographic factors are much more important than financial factors in the determination of the elderly's living arrangements.

Summary

The binomial probit results indicate that high levels of home equity encourage housing changes that reduce equity, while high levels of financial assets deter home equity reduction. The results for income variables are mixed, although evidence is presented suggesting that income deters equity reduction at the same time that it promotes mobility. Demographic variables describing retirement, marital, and health status are found to play large and significant roles in the regressions. The magnitude of their coefficients dwarf those of the financial variables.

Similar results are found in the multinomial logit regressions. High levels of home equity are found to encourage moves to homes of less equity and rental units. High asset levels deter moves to rental units and encourage moves that increase equity. The results for income variables are also mixed in these analyses. Again it is found that demographic variables dominate the regressions, and that their effects are alternative specific. Retirement plays a large role in moves into rental units and dependency, but is not as important for other alternatives. Being married is found to deter moves into rental units, and becoming widowed is found to promote moves into dependency and rental situations. Physical limitation plays a large role in moves into dependent living arrangements.

Discussion and Conclusion

The analyses provide some degree of evidence that is consistent with the theory that financial factors play a role in the housing decisions of older homeowners. However the results are not robust across specifications and various empirical techniques.

The results pertaining to demographic effects are robust across specifications and techniques. Coefficients on marital, retirement, and health status are found to be relatively large and significant in almost all of the analyses. Variables describing age, gender, and children also enter significantly in some instances.

The conclusions implied by these results are that while financial factors are likely to play a role in the elderly's housing decisions, demographic factors are much more important.

APPENDIX A
Descriptions of Explanatory Variables

I.   Housing Costs
    A.   Whether Mortgage - A dummy variable equal to 1 if the household has a mortgage on its home, 0 if not.
    B.   Mortgage Payment - Annual mortgage payments in thousands of 1987 dollars.
    C.   Property Tax - Annual property tax paid on home in thousands of 1987 dollars.
    D.   Utilities - The sum of annual total utility payments in thousands of 1987 dollars.

II. Housing Characteristics
    A.   Rooms - Total number of rooms in the home not including bathrooms.
    B.   DU Type - A dummy variable equal to 1 if the home is a single-family unit, and 0 if it is a multi-unit structure, mobile home, or trailer.
    C.   Yrs in Home - The number of years that the household has lived in the current home. The variable is accurate to within one year for tenures beginning after 1964. Before that, only bracket ranges are available: If current tenure began between 1959 and 1963, 1961 is used to calculate length; if between 1958 and 1954, 1956 is used; if between 1953 and 1944, 1948 is used. Those with tenures beginning before 1944 are assumed to have moved in as of 1938.

III. Financial
    A.   Home Equity - House value net of remaining mortgage principle in thousands of 1987 dollars.
    B.   Assets - For the binomial probit analyses, asset levels are "grossed up" from asset income using the following procedure: All households were assumed to have $200 in non-interest bearing assets. The first $100 in asset income was assumed to come from assets with a 5% return. Asset income above this amount was assumed to come from assets with a 10% return. This variable is also in thousands of

1987 dollars. More sophisticated techniques are used for the multinomial logit analyses, and these are explained in the text.

C. Taxable Income - Non-asset taxable income in thousands of 1987 dollars.

D. Transfer Income - All transfer income except help from relatives in thousands of 1987 dollars.

IV. Demographic

A. Age - Age of the head of household in years.

B. Female - A dummy variable equal to 1 if the head of household is female, 0 if not.

C. College - A dummy variable equal to 1 if the head of household has a college degree, 0 if not.

D. Retired - A dummy variable equal to 1 if the head is retired or permanently disabled, 0 if not.

E. Become Retired - A dummy variable equal to 1 if the head is working in the initial year and retired or permanently disabled in the next.

F. Married - A dummy variable equal to 1 if the head is married in the initial year.

G. Become Widowed - A dummy variable equal to 1 if the head is married in the initial year and widowed in the next.

H. Limited - A subjective dummy variable equal to 1 if the head is limited by a physical condition.

I. Become Limited - A dummy variable equal to 1 if the head is healthy in the initial year and limited in the next.

J. Kids - A dummy variable equal to 1 if the household contains children.

K. Kids Leave - A dummy variable equal to 1 if the number of children declines between the initial year and the next year.

L. Rels Help - A dummy variable equal to 1 if the household receives money from relatives, 0 if not.

M. Amt Rels Help - The yearly amount of help received from relatives in thousands of 1987 dollars.

V. A DYNAMIC PROGRAMING ANALYSIS

The analyses of the previous chapter do not completely capture the dynamic, forward-looking optimization problem that the elderly face when making housing decisions. This chapter specifies households' housing decisions as a dynamic programing problem and estimates their utility parameters regarding housing. The chapter is organized as follows: The first section describes in general how dynamic programing techniques can be used to uncover preferences. The following section specifies the state and control variables used, and the functional form of the utility function to be estimated in this context. A third section presents estimates of the beliefs of the households, and the fourth presents the estimates of households' utility parameters. A final section critiques the results and suggests future enhancements to the model.

THE DYNAMIC PROGRAMING MODEL

This section explains the use of dynamic programing to estimate the housing preferences of the elderly. It begins with an explanation of dynamic programing and then describes how it can be used to uncover a household's preferences.

The Theory of Dynamic Programing

In its simplest form, dynamic programing can be thought of as the intertemporal optimal choice of a control variable c_t, given stochastic state variables s_t. In utility analysis, the economic agent selects c_t from time 0 to terminal time T to maximize expected lifetime utility. Mathematically this is written as (Bertsekas, (1976)):

$$(5.1) \quad \underset{c_t}{\text{Max}} \ E \left[\sum_0^T \beta^t \ U(\theta, c_t, s_t) \right] \quad \text{s.t.} \quad E[s_{t+1}] = f(s_t, c_t)$$

where β is a discount rate and θ represents utility function parameters. Usually in these contexts c_t stands for consumption and $f(\cdot)$ stands for a set of stochastic budget constraints.

A problem such as this almost never has an obvious solution. This is true both because of the randomness of the state variables and because the choice of c_t that maximizes the single period utility $U(\theta, c_t, s_t)$ will not in general maximize the entire sum of utilities from 0 to T: The choice of c_t in time t will affect utility in later periods via the constraint. Thus the choice of c_t must be made considering its effect on future utility.

The solution to these sorts of problems usually requires that special mathematical techniques be used. One such technique is known as backward induction, and uses what Bellman (1957) calls the "principle of optimality". The basic idea is that the intertemporal optimization problem can be solved by starting with the last period and moving backwards. In the final period the economic agent will solve

$$(5.2) \qquad \underset{c_T}{\text{Max}}\ U(\theta, c_T, s_T) \qquad \text{given } s_T \qquad .$$

The solution to this will generally not be a specific value but rather a rule that specifies an optimal value of c_T for every s_T. Once this rule is defined, expression (5.2) can be described as a value function:

$$(5.3) \qquad V_T(\theta, c, s)\ =\ \underset{c_T}{\text{Max}}\ U(\theta, c_T, s_T) \qquad .$$

Once the value function is defined for time T, the optimization problem for time T-1 can be addressed:

$$(5.4) \qquad \underset{c_{T-1}}{\text{Max}}\left[U(\theta, c_{T-1}, s_{T-1})\ +\ \beta \cdot E[V_T(\theta, c, s)] \right] \qquad \text{given } s_{T-1} \quad .$$

Here the control variable will be chosen not only for its effect on current utility, but also for its effect on the value function. This process of updating the value function backwards through time is continued until the formula for time 0 is derived:

$$(5.5) \quad \underset{c_0}{\text{Max}} \left[U(\theta,c_0,s_0) \; + \; \beta \cdot E[V_1(\theta,c,s)] \right] \qquad \text{given } s_0$$

where the value function is the sum of the discounted utilities from time 1 to T.

While this procedure is a useful way to describe the optimization problem, the computational complexity of the problem can be very large. To solve it one must typically evaluate all combinations of the possible levels of c_t over all T time periods, and over the probability distribution of the state variables. One can easily see that problems where c_t can assume many values over a long time period are very complex. Until recently computer technology limited the complexity of the problems that could be solved in this manner. However with the increasing availability of high-speed computers the complexity of the feasible problems has greatly increased.

Estimation of Preferences Using Dynamic Programing

The technique described in the earlier section describes how one can model the intertemporal decisions of an economic agent. However the primary purpose of this chapter is to use dynamic programing techniques to uncover the preferences of economic agents. To this end it is assumed that agents behave as if they solve the dynamic programing problem, and by observing this behavior it is possible to estimate the preferences that cause them to take their actions. Thus the estimation procedure can be thought of as a complex revealed preference problem.

As in the previous section, the analysis begins with a description of the control and state variables, c_t and s_t respectively. A framework described in Phelan and Rust (1991) is used, where s_t is decomposed into observed state variables x_t and unobserved state variables ε_t. It is assumed that the evolution of these state variables over time is independent of contemporaneously observed state variables, and can be described by the following probability equation (Rust, (1989)):

(5.6) $\Pi(x_{t+1},\varepsilon_{t+1}|x_t,\varepsilon_t,c_t) = p(x_{t+1}|x_t,c_t) \cdot q(\varepsilon_{t+1}|x_{t+1})$

where $q(\cdot)$ is a non-identical multivariate extreme value distribution. It is also assumed that the realizations of ε_t are independent across persons, time, and choice of value for control variable. For econometric reasons it is necessary that ε_t has dimension equal to the dimension of the choice set for the control variables. These assumptions enable the specification of an empirically tractable likelihood function over the estimated utility parameter vector θ (Rust, (1989)):

$$(5.7) \qquad L(\theta) = \prod_{i=1}^{I} \prod_{t=1}^{T} P(\theta,c_t^i|x_t^i) \cdot p(x_t^i|x_{t-1}^i,c_{t-1}^i)$$

where (because of the assumption of the extreme value distribution, with t and i notation suppressed),

$$(5.8) \quad P(\theta,c|x) = \frac{\exp[U(\theta,x,c)+\beta \cdot E(V(\theta,x,c))]}{\sum_C \exp[U(\theta,x,c)+\beta \cdot E(V(\theta,x,c))]}$$

and where the expectation operators in (5.8) refer to the $p(\cdot)$ probabilities of (5.6), and C is the entire set of values from which c may be chosen. Intuitively, expression (5.8) means that the probability of a household choosing a particular alternative can be expressed as a ratio of the utility derived from the alternative over the sum of utilities derived from all alternatives.

The estimation procedure proceeds as follows: (1) The $p(\cdot)$ transitions are estimated separately, and are taken as given in the likelihood function. (2) Given an initial value of the vector θ, the derivatives of (5.7) with respect to the θ vector are calculated. (3) Using these derivatives and an approximation of the hessian matrix, a new value of θ is calculated. The process is repeated until a convergence criteria is met. In this way the estimation technique is completely analogous to Newton's well-known iterative estimation method (Judge et al., (1982)).

VARIABLE AND MODEL SPECIFICATION

This section describes the specific state and control variables used in the dynamic programing estimation, and specifies the functional form for the utility function whose parameters will be estimated.

State Variables

The computational complexity of the dynamic programing estimation technique requires economy with the factors used as state variables in this analysis. Those factors that seem to be the most important and interesting from the results of the previous empirical chapters are chosen. The number of categories for each variable are also kept rather small. The observed state vector is specified as follows:

(5.9) $x_t = (hs_t, as_t, ys_t, rs_t, ls_t, ms_t, a_t)$ where

hs_t is housing status ($1987), with

hs_t = 1 if own a home with equity ($66,000, +\infty$)
2 if own a home with equity ($44,000, $66,000]
3 if own a home with equity ($22,000, $44,000]
4 if own a home with equity ($-\infty$, $22,000]
5 if rent
6 if live in a dependent living arrangement

as_t is imputed financial asset level (1987$), with

as_t = 1 if financial assets (0, $200]
2 if financial assets ($200, $20,000]
3 if financial assets ($20,000, $40,000]
4 if financial assets ($40,000, $60,000]
5 if financial assets ($60,000, +\infty$)

ys_t is total non-asset income (1987$), with

ys_t = 1 if income ($-\infty$, $5,000]
2 if income ($5,000, $10,000]
3 if income ($10,000, $15,000]
4 if income ($15,000, $20,000]
5 if income ($20,000, +\infty$)

rs_t is retirement status, with
$$rs_t = 1 \text{ if the head is retired or permanently disabled}$$
$$0 \text{ if not}$$

ls_t is limitation status, with
$$ls_t = 2 \text{ if the head is dead}$$
$$1 \text{ if the head is physically limited}$$
$$0 \text{ if not}$$

ms_t is marital status, with
$$ms_t = 1 \text{ if the head is married}$$
$$0 \text{ if not}$$

a_t is age, with a_t = the age of the head minus 50: [0,50].

Even this rather coarse specification allows x_t to take on 60,000 separate values.

The Control Variable
    In this initial specification, the primary concern is with the utility that the household receives from the various housing arrangements. For the time being the utility from ordinary consumption will be suppressed. Thus the control variable is one dimensional, and describes the housing choice made by the household:

hd_t is the housing decision, with
hd_t = 1 if stay in or move into a home with equity
    ($66,000, +∞)
    2 if stay in or move into a home with equity
    ($44,000, $66,000]
    3 if stay in or move into a home with equity
    ($22,000, $44,000]
    4 if stay in or move into a home with equity
    (-∞, $22,000]
    5 if stay in or move into a rental unit
    6 if stay in or move into a dependent living
    arrangement.

There are many cases in which a homeowner would be classified as moving from one home equity bracket to another even though no move or mortgage action is taken. This may occur because of appreciation or depreciation of the home's value, the gradual payment of mortgage principal, or simple reporting errors. It would be inappropriate to classify these households as making the same changes as those that move or acquire mortgages. It is therefore prudent to specify an own-to-own housing change to take place only if the homeowner moves to another home or acquires a mortgage during the previous year, and if the action places them in a different home equity bracket. All other continuing home-owners are assumed to stay in the housing state that they occupied in the previous period.

This specification of the control variable may not capture all of the housing change behavior of interest. For example, a homeowner who sells her $200,000 home to move into a different $100,000 home is making a significant housing change, but the specification above classifies her as choosing to remain in the same housing state as before the move. Likewise, households may move between different renting arrangements, or different dependent arrangements, and be classified the same as those making no change. Additionally there is no explicit housing state describing mortgage behavior. These problems could be dealt with by enriching the descriptions of the housing states. However, the addition of more housing states will greatly increase the computational complexity of the problem, and thus it is reserved for future work.

Utility Function Specification

To complete the specification of the dynamic programing estimation problem, the functional form of the single-period utility function must also be specified. The specification described below suppresses the utility from consumption, but is very general in the way it treats utility from housing status:

(5.10) $U(hs, hd, as, ys, rs, ls, ms, a) =$

$$\sum_{i=1}^{6} \left[\alpha_i \cdot I\{hs = i\} \quad + \quad I\{hs = i\} \cdot \right.$$

$$\left. [\beta_{i1}(as) + \beta_{i2}(ys) + \beta_{i3}(rs) + \beta_{i4}(ls) + \beta_{i5}(ms) + \beta_{i6}(a)/10] \right] .$$

In the second line of (5.10), the parameters of interest are the six α_i's, which represent the baseline utilities associated with the six housing states defined above. Each of these measures is "shifted" by the parameters on the six state variables in the third line of (5.10). These parameters represent how financial and demographic variables affect the utility received from each of the housing alternatives. For instance if $\beta_{16} < 0$, then there is evidence that advanced age decreases the utility received from living in a home with equity greater than \$66,000.

ESTIMATION OF BELIEFS

This section reports the estimates of the transition probabilities of equation (5.6). The section is named "estimation of beliefs" because households' subjective beliefs about the evolution of their state variables are assumed to equal to the empirically observable transition probabilities for the state variables. The assumption is much like the rational expectations assumption in macro-economics. First the construction of the transition matrix from marginal matrices is described, and then each of the marginal matrices is estimated.

Decomposition and Exclusion Restrictions

Because x_t may take on any of 60,000 values, direct estimation of the probability transition matrix with even the largest of data sets is infeasible. Instead the analysis takes advantage of various properties of the state variables and a well-known law of probability to simplify the estimation of the transition matrix.

First, it is noted that the age state variable is not random, but that $a_{t+1} = a_t + 1$ with probability equal to 1. It is also assumed that the housing state variable is perfectly controlled by the household, so that $hs_{t+1} = hd_t$ with probability equal to 1. This simplifies the remaining problem by reducing the dimensionality of the matrix to be estimated.

The remaining state variables are assumed to depend on one another, and make up the probability matrix to be estimated:

(5.11) $p(as_{t+1}, ys_{t+1}, rs_{t+1}, ls_{t+1}, ms_{t+1} \mid as_t, ys_t, rs_t, ls_t, ms_t, hs_t, a_t)$.

This expression can be simplified by decomposing it into the product of each argument's marginal probability. Certain conditioning arguments are also excluded to avoid spurious causality and to simplify estimation. After decomposition and exclusion restrictions, the following expression equivalent to (5.11) is derived:

(5.12) $p(as_{t+1} \mid as_t, ys_t, rs_t, ls_t, ms_t, a_t, \{ls_{t+1} \neq 2\})$ ·

$p(ys_{t+1} \mid ys_t, rs_t, ls_t, ms_t, a_t, \{ls_{t+1} \neq 2\})$ ·

$p(rs_{t+1} \mid rs_t, ls_t, ms_t, a_t, \{ls_{t+1} \neq 2\})$ ·

$p(ls_{t+1} \mid ls_t, ms_t, a_t, \{ls_{t+1} \neq 2\})$ ·

$p(ms_{t+1} \mid ms_t, a_t, \{ls_{t+1} \neq 2\})$ ·

$p(\{ls_{t+1} \neq 2\} \mid ls_t, a_t)$

In the following subsections each of these marginal probability matrices are taken up in reverse order. Each component is estimated using all cross sections in the Panel Study of Income Dynamics (PSID) that contain the necessary data.

Remaining Alive
    The first transition estimated is whether the head of household continues to live from one period to the next $\{ls_{t+1} \neq 2\}$. The results of a binomial logit regression are presented in Table 5.1. The dependent variable in this regression equals 1 if the head of household remains alive into the following year. The negative coefficients on the physical limitation dummy and age indicate that limitation and advancing age reduce the probability that the head remains alive. Marital status is not included in this regression out of fear that the deaths of married heads might be more frequently reported than the deaths of single heads. This could lead to the spurious conclusion that being married causes death. Rather than complicating matters by attempting to adjust for potential bias, marital status is merely omitted from this regression.

Table 5.1 - Living Probability Estimation Results
(Dependent variable = 1 if alive in next period)

Variable	Coefficient	t-statistic
Constant	5.35	33.411
Limited	-0.988	-7.821
Age	-0.0355	-5.574

# of observations = 19439
-log likelihood = 1608.648

Marital Status

The probabilities associated with marital status transitions are estimated next. Again a binomial logit regression is specified with the dependent variable equal to 1 if the head of household is married in the following year. The results of this regression are presented in Table 5.2. The increase in sample size is due to the fact that for one of the waves physical limitation is not recorded. The inclusion of this cross section more than makes up for the decrease in sample size by excluding those who die (conditioning on $\{ls_{t+1} \neq 2\}$). The results indicate that change between marital states is infrequent: Households that start off married tend to continue to be married, and those that are not married are even more likely to remain so. Age has a relatively small negative effect on the probability of being married.

Table 5.2 - Marital Status Estimation Results
(Dependent variable = 1 if married in next period)

Variable	Coefficient	t-statistic
Constant	-4.23	-30.369
Married	7.80	63.544
Age	-0.0387	-7.712

# of observations = 20776
-log likelihood = 2497.172

Limitation Status

The analysis now turns to the transitions associated with physical limitation status. The dependent variable in this regression is equal to 1 if the head of household is physically limited in the following year, 0 if not. The explanatory variables are limitation in the current year, marital status in the current year, and age. Excluding observations with missing values yields a sample of 19012. The results of the regression are presented in Table 5.3.

Table 5.3 - Limitation Status Estimation Results
(Dependent variable = 1 if limited in next period)

Variable	Coefficient	t-statistic
Constant	-1.87	-33.466
Limited	3.19	80.499
Married	-0.188	-4.721
Age	0.0248	10.372

# of observations = 19012
-log likelihood = 8434.042

As in the case of marital status, one's limitation status in the following year is very much dependent on one's current status. Being married tends to reduce the probability that a head of household is limited, while age tends to increase it.

Retirement Status

The final demographic factor explored in this manner is the retirement status of the head of household. Again the problem is specified as a binomial logit regression, with the dependent variable equal to 1 if the head is retired or permanently disabled in the following year. The explanatory variables are age and retirement, limitation, and marital status in the current year. The results of this regression are presented in Table 5.4.

The results are generally what one would expect. Being retired in the current year makes it very likely that a head

Table 5.4 - Retirement Status Estimation Results
(Dependent Variable = 1 if retired in next period)

Variable	Coefficient	t-statistic
Constant	-2.59	-40.370
Retired	3.33	75.257
Limited	0.542	12.198
Married	0.564	12.315
Age	0.0478	17.585

# of observations = 19094
-log likelihood = 7330.738

will be retired the following year. Physical limitation also seems to encourage retirement, although its effect is not as great. Curiously, being married appears to encourage retirement, the opposite of what one might expect. This may be the result of a bias similar to that described in the limitation section. Finally, age has a fairly strong positive effect on the probability that a head of household will be retired. Future work will deal with the potential bias in this regression, and will utilize age categories rather than having age enter linearly.

Income
The analysis now turns to the transition probabilities of the households' non-asset income in the following year. Because income status can assume five different values, a single binomial logit regression is not appropriate. Attempts to estimate five separate binomial logits for each income category yield results that violate probability laws. Therefore a single multinomial logit specification is estimated. Ideally one would like to include dummy variables describing the income state in the current year in the set of explanatory variables. However when dummy variables indicating income category 4 or income category 5 are included in the regression, the iterative estimation procedure will not converge. Therefore the income category (1,2,3,4,5) and its square are included directly in the multinomial logit income regressions.

Table 5.5 - Income Estimation Results
(Dependent variable = income category in next period)
(t-stats in parentheses)

	Category 1	Category 2	Category 3	Category 4
Constant	7.59	2.81	-4.82	-9.70
	(17.3)	(6.15)	(-10.1)	(-16.3)
Income	-3.74	1.16	5.48	6.86
	(-13.5)	(4.26)	(19.7)	(21.3)
Income Squared	0.265	-0.520	-1.03	-1.06
	(6.63)	(-13.0)	(-26.6)	(-25.2)
Retired	0.593	0.799	0.760	0.821
	(5.61)	(8.26)	(8.22)	(9.45)
Limited	0.996	0.601	0.275	0.151
	(10.2)	(6.81)	(3.23)	(1.84)
Married	-1.71	-1.34	-0.764	-0.571
	(-16.3)	(-14.5)	(-8.52)	(-6.49)
Age	0.0511	0.0494	0.0268	0.0162
	(7.75)	(8.00)	(4.43)	(2.76)

# of observations = 18934
-log likelihood = 16356.708

The results are presented in Table 5.5. Recall that the coefficients should be interpreted as relative to the null group, income category 5. Generally the income variables perform as expected, with coefficients that imply high probabilities of staying in the same category or moving to adjacent categories. Being retired or physically limited raises the probability that a household will be in the lower income categories, as does advancing age. Being married reduces the probability of being in lower income categories, probably because there are two potential wage earners in a couple, and that transfer benefits are greater for couples.

While the coefficients in the previous regression seem quite reasonable, they may not adequately describe the empirically observable log-normal distribution of income. Future work will utilize the log-normal estimation technique of Rust (1990), or the nonparametric method of Bird (1991).[1]

Table 5.6 - Asset Estimation Results
(Dependent variable = asset category in next period)
(t-stats in parentheses)

	Category 1	Category 2	Category 3	Category 4
Constant	9.11	1.11	-2.31	-3.53
	(29.7)	(3.53)	(-6.62)	(-8.44)
Asset	-2.73	2.11	3.52	3.46
	(-17.4)	(13.0)	(20.0)	(16.2)
Asset Squared	0.164	-0.609	-0.702	-0.597
	(6.49)	(-22.1)	(-25.6)	(-19.3)
Income	-0.353	0.299	0.108	-0.0520
	(-2.25)	(1.91)	(0.65)	(-0.30)
Income Squared	-0.0287	-0.0759	-0.0429	-0.0185
	(-1.17)	(-3.13)	(-1.68)	(-0.70)
Retired	-0.324	-0.323	-0.175	-0.246
	(-3.66)	(-3.74)	(-1.94)	(-2.63)
Limited	0.406	0.129	0.109	0.134
	(4.85)	(1.57)	(1.28)	(1.51)
Married	0.156	-0.0572	0.0350	0.110
	(1.68)	(-0.63)	(0.37)	(1.11)
Age	-0.0577	-0.0108	-0.0114	-0.0167
	(-10.6)	(-2.02)	(-2.02)	(-2.84)

# of observations = 18934
-log likelihood = 15008.499

Asset Level
Asset transitions are estimated analogously to those for income, in a multinomial logit framework. To the list of variables appearing in the income regression, asset category (1,2,3,4,5) and its square are added. The results are presented in Table 5.6.

The results of Table 5.6 are generally what is expected. The asset variables imply that households are most likely to remain in the same asset category or move into one directly adjacent. The coefficients on income do not reveal any strong pattern, but generally it appears as though high levels of income reduce the probability of being in a low asset category. Being retired seems to reduce the probability of being in low asset categories, while being physically limited increases it. No clear pattern emerges from the coefficients on marital status, while advanced age appears to reduce the probability that a household is in a low asset category.

PREFERENCE ESTIMATION

In this section the dynamic programing techniques described in above are employed to estimate the utility parameters of the utility function (5.10) given that the households have beliefs described by the estimation techniques of the previous section.

Estimation and Interpretation
As with the case of standard multinomial logit regression, all of the utility parameters will not be econometrically identified. Thus it is necessary to omit one of the housing categories from the estimation, and interpret the coefficients as relative to what they are for the omitted category. To make the interpretation of the coefficients as easy as possible, the highest home equity owning category is omitted from the estimation.

Table 5.7 presents the results of the initial dynamic programing estimation. In each column of the table the utility parameters associated with a particular housing state are presented. The first line of each column repre-

Table 5.7
Results From Dynamic Programing Estimation
(t-stats in parentheses)

Coefficient	Housing State 2	Housing State 3	Housing State 4
α	1.67	3.70	4.92
	(8.75)	(20.7)	(26.1)
β_{*1} (assets)	-0.297	-0.578	-1.02
	(-10.5)	(-19.9)	(-28.3)
β_{*2} (income)	-0.243	-0.568	-0.784
	(-5.57)	(-13.3)	(-17.2)
β_{*3} (retired)	-0.0302	-0.233	-0.558
	(-0.238)	(-1.87)	(-4.17)
β_{*4} (limited)	0.0315	0.178	0.365
	(0.246)	(1.45)	(2.77)
β_{*5} (married)	-0.237	0.115	0.315
	(-2.19)	(1.12)	(2.92)
β_{*6} (age)	0.0112	-0.128	-0.128
	(0.205)	(-2.46)	(-2.31)

discount rate = .95
# of observations = 12323
-log likelihood = 18438.012
gradient*direction = 9.68 E-7

Table 5.7 – continued
Results From Dynamic Programing Estimation
(t-stats in parentheses)

Coefficient	Housing State 5	Housing State 6
α	5.66 (33.2)	3.60 (13.8)
β_{*1} (assets)	-0.948 (-31.7)	-1.11 (-17.5)
β_{*2} (income)	-0.650 (-15.8)	-1.10 (-13.3)
β_{*3} (retired)	0.229 (1.88)	0.209 (1.11)
β_{*4} (limited)	0.405 (3.31)	0.959 (4.86)
β_{*5} (married)	-1.03 (-10.4)	-0.863 (-5.38)
β_{*6} (age)	-0.488 (-9.75)	0.0913 (1.36)

discount rate = .95
# of observations = 12323
-log likelihood = 18438.012
gradient*direction = 9.68 E-7

sents the baseline utility received from living in that housing alternative. The next six values represent the coefficients for the variables that shift the utility for each housing alternative.

The reader should not interpret the coefficients as describing directly observable levels of utility. In this context it is not possible to say anything about the absolute level of utility for any housing arrangement, only that the utility received is greater or smaller than the utility in another arrangement.

When looking at Table 5.7, one should not interpret the positive baseline utilities for the five estimated housing alternatives as an indication that these alternatives provide more satisfaction than the housing alternative that is omitted. The utility levels are appropriately interpreted *only* in the context of realized values for the financial and demographic variables. Likewise, it is not appropriate to interpret a negative coefficient as an indication that a higher value for a variable reduces the utility from a given housing alternative. Rather, it reduces the utility *relative* to the utility for the omitted alternative.

Some Illustrative Examples

Perhaps the best way to introduce the reader to what these coefficients mean is through illustrative examples. This is accomplished by creating example households and comparing their relative single-period utility levels among housing states.

The first description is of a poor, fairly young, working household. It is assumed that it falls into the lowest asset and income categories, and that the head of household is working, not physically limited, married, and is 60 years of age. The relative utilities among the housing states for this household are presented in Table 5.8.

In this table the utility that this household receives from owning a house with the highest category of home equity is fixed at 0. (Any number could have been chosen because the *relative* utilities that are of interest.) The housing alternative with the highest utility for this household is owning a home in the lowest equity bracket. The utilities

Table 5.8
Relative Utility Levels: Example 1

Household Description	Housing Category	Relative Utility
Asset Level 1	1	0
Income Level 1	2	0.905
Working	3	2.536
Not Limited	4	3.305
Married	5	2.544
60 Years Old	6	0.611

from owning in the next highest equity bracket or from renting are relatively close to this level. The satisfaction received from living dependently or owning a home in the second highest equity level are quite a bit lower, but are still higher than that which would be received from the highest home equity ownership category.

The next example depicts a wealthy retired household. It is assumed that this household has income and assets that fall in the highest categories. The head of household is retired, not physically limited, is married, and is 75 years old. The relative utilities for this household are presented in Table 5.9.

Table 5.9
Relative Utility Levels: Example 2

Household Description	Housing Category	Relative Utility
Asset Level 5	1	0
Income Level 5	2	-1.348
Retired	3	-2.474
Not Limited	4	-4.662
Married	5	-4.352
75 Years Old	6	-7.912

Again the utility for owning a home in the highest home equity bracket is set equal to 0. Please note that these numbers are in no way comparable to those in the earlier table, because now the baseline utility is defined to be 0 for an entirely different type of household. Because all of the utilities associated with the other housing options are negative, it is clear that owning at the highest equity level is associated with the highest satisfaction for this household. The next closest levels would be achieved by owning in the next highest equity categories. The lowest degree of satisfaction for this household comes from living in a dependent situation.

Next the relative utilities for a very old physically limited household are examined. It is assumed that this household falls into the lowest income and asset categories, and is headed by a single, retired, physically limited person of age 90. The relative utilities associated with this household are presented below.

Table 5.10
Relative Utility Levels: Example 3

Household Description	Housing Category	Relative Utility
Asset Level 1	1	0
Income Level 1	2	1.177
Retired	3	1.982
Limited	4	2.413
Not Married	5	2.743
90 Years Old	6	2.917

As with the two previous tables, utility in housing category 1 is set equal to 0 for this household. The highest level of satisfaction to be had for this household is from living in a dependent arrangement. Utility levels very close to this can be achieved by renting. The home ownership categories are below these levels, with the utility declining as home equity is larger. The closeness of the utility levels between renting and dependency suggest that dependent living arrangements may only be best for those households who are very old and sick, and have very little in the way of financial resources.

The final example household examined is less extreme than the three previous ones. The household falls in the second highest asset category, and the middle income category. The household is also retired, healthy, married, and 65 years of age. The relative utilities associated with these characteristics are presented in Table 5.11.

Table 5.11
Relative Utility Levels: Example 4

Household Description	Housing Category	Relative Utility
Asset Level 2	1	0
Income Level 3	2	0.099
Retired	3	0.524
Not Limited	4	0.095
Married	5	0.280
65 Years Old	6	-2.455

For this household the greatest utility level is achieved by owning a home in the second home equity bracket. However the differences between the other independent living arrangements are very small, indicating near indifference between the alternatives. Only the dependent living arrangement is clearly inferior, having a very negative relative utility.

A few comments are necessary before continuing with the interpretation of the results. One should not think that results above imply that households will constantly switch between housing arrangements to always be in the housing arrangement that provides the highest level of single-period utility. The difference in utilities must be great enough and sustained over a long enough period to make a costly housing change optimal. Attempts to estimate the transition costs in terms of utility have to date been unsuccessful.

Work continues to find a specification that is informative and converges.

Some readers may be tempted to criticize the results along the following lines: They may think it self-evident that anyone is best off in the largest and most expensive of owner-occupied homes. However for those that have low levels of income and assets the cost of upkeep and property taxes may be so large that basic necessities are not affordable. In this case it would be optimal to sell the home and move to less costly arrangements.

Discussion of Parameter Estimates

While the previous section familiarizes the reader with this estimation framework, it does little to describe the effects of specific factors on households utility from the various housing arrangements. It is in this section that these considerations are examined.

The age of the head of household is considered first. It appears as though advancing age causes a polarization in the elderly's choice of housing arrangements: Relative to owning in the highest equity bracket, age tends to decrease the utility received from owning at low levels of equity and renting. Age appears to have very little effect on the utility from dependency (relative to the omitted category). This suggests that as age increases, households tend to enjoy high equity home ownership and dependent living conditions more than the other alternatives.

Marital status also appears to play a significant role in the utility garnered from various housing arrangements. There appears to be no strong marriage effect on utility among the ownership alternatives. However the large negative coefficients for the renting and dependency alternatives indicate that married households receive more utility from all types of owner-occupied arrangements.

Physical limitation also appears to effect the utility of housing arrangements. Relative to the high home equity omitted group, physical limitation increases the utility received from lower equity ownership. This pattern becomes stronger as the level of home equity falls, although it is only statistically significant in the lowest equity cat-egory. The effect is even stronger for the rental alternative, and is strongest for dependent living arrangements. This observation may be the result of the high cost and physical dependency produced by the limitation causing the household to liquidate home equity.

Retirement status appears to have an effect on utility similar to that of increasing age. Relative to the omitted category, being retired seems to increase the utility a household receives from renting and from dependency. At the same time, retirement appears to decrease the utility from owning a home with lower levels of home equity.

Perhaps the most dramatic of results are the values for the coefficients on income and assets. The coefficients on both these factors are large and of high statistical significance. Their negative signs indicate that relative to the omitted category, high levels of both income and assets reduce the utility derived from other arrangements. These effects become stronger at lower levels of home equity, suggesting that within the owning categories, high income and wealth increase the satisfaction from owning homes having high levels of home equity. The coefficients in the renting and dependency groups are generally of greater magnitude than the ownership groups, indicating that high levels of these financial variables make home ownership in general more favorable.

Before continuing with a discussion of the results, the reader should be aware that the t-statistics in Table 5.7 may be overstated. This occurs both because pooled cross-sectional data are used, and because they have not been adjusted for the variation that enters via the estimation of beliefs. Future work will adjust for the latter problem.

Discussion

These results are generally consistent with the results of the earlier empirical chapters and the mathematical theory of chapter 2. Retirement, health, and marital status all appear to play a significant role in the elderly's housing decisions. High levels of income and financial assets again appear to encourage home ownership, and to deter moves to rental and dependent arrangements.

However the results of this chapter differ from the earlier results in important ways. Most noticeably, financial variables play a large role in these regressions whereas their role in the earlier analyses is limited. This may be a result of the different structure of the regressions: The previous ones focus on housing changes while this chapter focuses on housing states. The financial variables may play a large role in the selection of initial housing states but be less important in influencing subsequent housing changes.

Secondly, the classification of homeowners into multiple groups along home equity levels reveals that combining all homeowners into one group may be inappropriate. Merely controlling for home equity as is done in chapter 4 may not be enough if demographic effects cause differing responses from homeowners with differing levels of home equity.

CRITIQUE AND FUTURE ENHANCEMENTS

The procedures of the earlier sections are subject to a number of criticisms. This section will discuss the most important of these and suggest ways in which they can be treated.

Inadequate Utility Function

The utility function described by (5.10) is not complete for a number of reasons. One of the simplest enhancements is to include a term describing the utility cost of making a change in housing status. This could be achieved by adding a term such as

$$(5.13) \qquad \sum_{i=1}^{6} \sum_{j=1}^{6} \gamma_{ij} \cdot I\{hs=i, hd=j\}$$

to equation (5.10). Here the γ's represent the utility change from going to one housing state to another. Although initial work with this specification indicates that the explanatory power may be greatly improved, convergence has been elusive.

Perhaps the most serious problem with this analysis is that the single-period utility function concentrates only on utility from housing and contains nothing describing the utility from ordinary consumption. Specifying a functional form for this is simple: One merely has to add an acceptable function for utility from consumption (such as log or quadratic) to equation (5.10).

However accurately measuring consumption is less simple, because the PSID does not contain a comprehensive measure of consumption. One alternative is to follow Hall and Mishkin (1982) by using the PSID's data for consumption of food as a imperfect proxy for total consumption. Another alternative is to follow the work of Phelan and Rust (1991) concerning retirement behavior and use utility of income as a replacement for the utility of consumption. However in this analysis housing decisions are unlikely to affect income while they may substantially change consumption. Thus the critical tradeoff present in Phelan and Rust would be lacking if income were used in this situation.

A promising remedy for this problem is the imputation of consumption from variables in the PSID (including food consumption) by Skinner (1987). He uses total consumption data from the Consumer Expenditure Survey (CES) and uses variables common to both the CES and PSID. He reports very favorable results, with the regressions having R-squareds of over .75. Future work may utilize Skinner's results to impute consumption and include it in the model.

The utility function also lacks a bequest motive. Utility from bequests could be specified as a function of terminal financial assets and home equity. Home equity could even enter separately to determine whether there is a premium on the bequeathing of housing wealth. This factor may be important if the head of household has a spouse or children.

State Variables

The state variables included in this analysis are by no means exhaustive. Gender and number of children in the family unit are omitted, both of which may play a significant role in households' taste for housing. Also ignored are all measures of housing costs examined in the previous specification. Inclusion of these factors greatly increase the computational burden of the estimation problem, but should be included in a complete model nonetheless.

The housing status variable is also somewhat lacking. Specifically it does not explicitly define states associated with having a mortgage on the home. Augmentation of the housing state variable in this respect will not only increase the dimensionality of the state vector, but will also greatly increase the number of utility parameters to be estimated.

Excessive Exclusion Restrictions

The exclusion restrictions embodied in (5.12) are intended to simplify estimation, but could be criticized as excessive. For example, asset and income levels do not appear in the estimation of future health status, even though wealthy households probably can afford better health care. Also, and possibly more importantly, the housing state variable is not included as an explanatory variable in any of the transition estimations. Most likely it should appear in the regression describing asset level transition, and, (if it is included in the future) housing cost.

Summary and Conclusion

The results of this chapter generally support the theory presented in chapter 2 and concur with the earlier empirical analyses in chapter 4. They go further than this however, suggesting that financial variables may play a fairly large role in the choice of housing arrangements and that disaggregating homeowners by equity group may be important for the understanding of their housing decisions. However the many shortcomings of the estimations presented here make these conclusions somewhat tentative.

Even with the shortcomings of the model, dynamic programing estimation is still a promising technique. No other technique has come as close to capturing the intertemporal optimization problem of households. With the improvements discussed in this section, this technique may yield even more interesting results regarding elderly households' preferences regarding home ownership.

NOTES

[1] First Rust assumes a log-normal distribution of income. Then the log of (continuous) income is regressed on a set of explanatory variables. Using the results of this regression he imputes an expected distribution of income in the following year given any set of values for the explanatory variables. By integrating the probability function over the various income brackets we can estimate the probability of falling within any of the brackets. Bird employs a similar procedure, only nonparametric regression is used to estimate the expected probability distribution. Either of these procedures is likely to be more accurate than the multinomial logit technique.

VI. SUMMARY AND
POLICY IMPLICATIONS

This work advances the knowledge regarding the housing decisions of elderly homeowners. The decision is a complex one, involving many factors. Previous work, as well as this one, has shown that home equity, housing characteristics, financial assets, income, marital status, retirement, health, the presence of children, psychological attachment, and transaction costs all play a role in the elderly's housing decision. One treatment such as this cannot hope to answer all the questions regarding the topic. However this work does contribute to the understanding of some of its aspects. This chapter describes the contribution, discusses its policy implications, and makes suggestions for future work.

SUMMARY OF RESULTS

Theoretic Results

The mathematical theory described in chapter 2 takes the viewpoint of a household that already resides in owner-occupied housing. It examines the housing alternatives that the homeowner faces: Move to a home with more equity, move to a home with smaller equity, liquidate home equity completely, acquire a new mortgage, or simply remain in the same home with no housing change. Thus the theory concentrates on the changes that the homeowner could make, rather than the determination of housing status. This is done due to the unique characteristics that home ownership gives to housing decisions, and because of the discrete and time-dependent nature of such decisions.

The theory improves understanding of the home equity decisions of elderly homeowners by integrating the financial and psychological factors affecting the housing decision into a unified framework. The model describes the tradeoff between the satisfaction that is provided by an owner-occupied home and the added consumption that liquidating the home equity could provide.

The comparative statics of chapter 2 provide testable hypotheses regarding the determinants of the elderly's housing decisions. They predict that high levels of home equity will (ceteris paribus) cause homeowners to desire to reduce home equity. They also predict that high levels of income and financial assets will deter such actions. Finally, the comparative statics predict that a higher level of satisfaction for home ownership and higher psychological moving costs will tend to deter housing changes that reduce home equity. The model provides a rigorous mathematical framework on which to base empirical analyses.

Empirical Results

The empirical results of this work are generally consistent with the theory presented in chapter 2. The binomial probit results of chapter 4 indicate that high levels of home equity are associated with an increased propensity to reduce home equity. Similarly, high levels of financial assets are negatively correlated with housing changes that reduce home equity. The evidence for the effect of income is weaker, because the positive effect of income on residential mobility may counteract its negative effect on equity reduction.

The binomial probit results also suggest that demographic factors and change in demographic factors have a strong effect on housing decisions. Marital status, retirement, and physical limitation, as well as changes in these factors are found to have a strong association with housing changes that reduce home equity. Moreover, these factors appear to play a much more important role in housing decisions than do financial factors.

The results of the multinomial logit analysis confirm and provide more detail than the binomial probit analysis. Again both financial and demographic factors appear to influence the housing decisions of the elderly, and demographic considerations appear to be more important. The most important contribution of the multinomial logit results is to show that all equity-reducing housing actions are not alike. Financial factors such as assets and home equity appear to influence moves where the household remains independent, and demographic factors have their greatest effect on housing changes that cause a tenure change. These results suggest that separating housing alternatives is an improvement over modeling the decision as a binary choice.

The dynamic programing estimation provides further evidence that both financial and demographic factors play important roles in housing decisions of the elderly. However, the analysis suggests that financial factors play a much larger role than that suggested by the earlier results. The dynamic programing results should be eyed with a bit more skepticism: The modeling of the utility function is crude and the omission of the utility costs of making housing changes effectively makes this an analysis of housing status, rather than of housing changes.

All of the empirical analyses are subject to some form of criticism. All make use of pooled cross-sectional data, which makes parameter estimates seem more precise than they actually are. The aggregation of alternatives inherent in the binomial probit analysis is shown by the multinomial logit approach to be inferior. However the disaggregation in the multinomial logit analysis necessitates the exclusion of several independent variables and of several observations with high levels of imputed assets. The dynamic programing analysis has conceptual advantages over the other empirical models, but has problems of its own: The "curse of dimensionality" forces limitations on the descriptive power of the explanatory variables used and on the richness of housing alternatives specified; and specifications that include the cost of housing change have to date eluded estimation.

POLICY IMPLICATIONS

The analyses described in this work seek to refine the scientific study of the home ownership decision of the elderly. Although it is not designed to be an examination of public policy, it has revealed some implications for the implementation of government programs. This section briefly discusses these implications.

Housing Costs

A number of government programs seek to aid the elderly and allow them to stay in their homes by reducing the burden of their housing expenses. These programs include heat and power bill subsidies, and deferral of property tax on owner-occupied homes until the time of sale. Although the programs no doubt improve the welfare of their participants, the results of chapter 4 suggest that they may have little effect on an elderly homeowner's ability to remain in the home. Perhaps the effect is only significant for a small group of owners who are financially constrained and have large expenses. If this is true the programs would not have much effect on those homeowners with sufficient financial resources or relatively low housing costs.

Social Security and Income Supplementation

Probably the government programs with the most effect on the elderly are Social Security and SSI. While most public policy interest has focused on these programs' effect on labor supply, the programs may also have an effect on housing decisions. There is some evidence in the empirical analyses to suggest that higher levels of income encourage homeowners to remain in owner-occupied housing. However other evidence suggests that higher income stimulates residential mobility and therefore housing changes. Also, there is fairly strong evidence to suggest that income inhibits moves to dependent living arrangements. While these observations may be true, the evidence here suggests that demographic effects are much more important than income.

Financial Instruments

The empirical results of this work are consistent with the notion that some older homeowners may wish to reduce home equity. They also reveal that housing changes are infrequent, possibly because of large psychological and financial costs to moving. In recent years it has been suggested that the elderly would be better off if they could somehow utilize their home equity without incurring the costs of moving. Homeowners that are still able to function in an independent setting and have a need for supplemental income would particularly stand to benefit from such an arrangement.

To this end financial instruments such as reverse annuity mortgages have been developed. As of this date, their effect is not widespread, perhaps because there is little demand for the instruments, or perhaps because there is a market failure of some sort: Financial intermediaries may be unwilling to assume the risk of letting homeowners stay in their homes until death, while the homeowner may be unwilling to risk eviction before she is ready to move. Since moral hazard and adverse selection problems may also be present, the market for such instruments may have failed.

If the market failure explanation, (rather than the lack of demand explanation), is true, there is a constructive role that government could take. Perhaps government guarantees of a modest return (much like the student loan program) could allow financial institutions to offer reverse mortgages at rates attractive enough to entice a large number of customers. A large scale program of reverse mortgages might provide enough pooling of risks to make the program feasible. The government could also alter tax laws to make these sorts of instruments more attractive.

However previous work indicates that the homeowners with the most to gain from such programs may be the ones that are in least need of such assistance. These programs will only provide substantial income to those with high levels of home equity. Since these sorts of homeowners often have high income and assets, they probably do not need the income as much as less wealthy homeowners. Also, given that much of the housing decision appears to depend more on demographic factors, there is reason to believe that in most cases such programs would have little impact on elderly homeowners' ability or desire to remain in their home. As in the case of housing cost subsidization, this type of program may only have its desired effect on the financially constrained independent elderly, and is more appropriately targeted only towards them.

FUTURE WORK

There remains much to be understood about the housing decisions of elderly homeowners. Perhaps the most important area to be studied is that of the cost of making housing changes. Understanding the extent to which these costs inhibit potentially utility-increasing housing changes is vital to a complete picture of the housing decisions of the elderly. Determining the source of these costs is also important. Appropriate economic modeling as well as appropriate public policy depends on whether the costs of housing change result from psychological attachment, or from financial constraints and market failures.

To guide public policy, future empirical work should focus on certain subpopulations of the elderly. Those who are income constrained, credit constrained and physically limited are likely to behave differently than the rest of elderly homeowners. Focusing attention on these groups would provide needed insight for the tailoring of public policy.

CONCLUSION

This book makcs a significant contribution to the literature on housing decisions of elderly homeowners. The decision is shown to be complex and to depend on a variety of financial and demographic factors.

There are many areas that remain unclear and that are fertile ground for further research. With an increasing percentage of the population nearing the age when they will make these decisions, a better understanding of the housing decisions of the elderly is clearly in order.

BIBLIOGRAPHY

Ai, Chunrong; Feinstein, Jonathan; McFadden, Daniel; and Pollakowski, Henry; "The Dynamics of Housing Demand by the Elderly: User Cost Effects," in *Issues in the Economics of Aging*, (D. Wise ed.), University of Chicago Press, 1990.

American Housing Survey 1985: National Core File Documentation, U.S. Department of Commerce, Bureau of the Census, 1987.

Artle, Roland, and Varaiya, Pravin, "Life Cycle Consumption and Homeownership," *Journal of Economic Theory* 18, pp 38-58, 1978.

Béland, Francois, "The Decision of Elderly Persons to Leave their Homes," *The Gerontologist* 24, pp 179-185, 1984.

Bellman, Richard, *Dynamic Programing*, Princeton Univ. Press, 1957.

Bertsekas, Dimitri, *Dynamic Programing and Stochastic Control*, Academic Press, 1976.

Bird, Edward J., "Tax-Transfer Policy and Income Risk," Unpublished Ph.D. Dissertation, Univ. of Wisconsin-Madison, 1991.

Boersch-Supan, Axel, "A Dynamic Analysis of Household Dissolution and Living Arrangement Transitions by Elderly Americans," NBER Working Paper #2808, January 1989.

Boersch-Supan, Axel; Hajivassiliou, Vassilis; Kotlikoff, Laurence; and Morris, John M.; "Health, Children, and Elderly Living Arrangements: A Multiperiod-Multinomial Probit Model with Unobserved Heterogeneity and Autocorrelated Errors," NBER Working Paper #3343, 1990.

Boersch-Supan, Axel; Kotlikoff, Laurence J.; and Morris, John N.; "The Dynamics of Living Arrangements of the Elderly," NBER Working Paper #2787, December 1988.

Danziger, Sheldon; Schwartz, Saul; and Smolensky, Eugene; "The Choice of Living Arrangements by the Elderly," in *Retirement and Economic Behavior*, (H. Aaron and G. Burtless eds.), Brookings Institute, 1984.

Ellwood, David, and Kane, Thomas, "The American Way of Aging: An Event History Analysis," NBER Working Paper #2892, March 1989.

Feinstein, Jonathan and McFadden, Daniel, "The Dynamics of Housing Demand by the Elderly: Wealth, Cash Flow, and Demographic Effects," NBER Working Paper #2471, December 1987.

Garber, Alan M., and MaCurdy, Thomas, "Nursing Home Utilization among the High-Risk Elderly," Hoover Institution Working Paper E-89-1, 1989.

Hall, Robert E., and Mishkin, Frederic S., "The Sensitivity of Consumption to Transitory Income: Estimates from Panel Data on Households," *Econometrica* 50, pp. 461-481, 1982.

Hobbs, Robert J., Keest, Kathleen, and DeWaal, Ian, "Consumer Problems with Home Equity Scams, Second Mortgages, and Home Equity Lines of Credit," AARP Public Policy Research Institute Paper C-23, July, 1989.

Hurd, Michael, "Wealth Depletion and Life Cycle Consumption by the Elderly," Unpublished Manuscript, September, 1990.

Judge, George C., Hill, R. Carter, Griffiths, William E., Lütkepohl, Helmut, Lee, Tsoung-Chao, *Introduction to the Theory and Practice of Econometrics*, John Wiley and Sons, 1982.

Kotlikoff, Laurence J., and Morris, John, "Why Don't the Elderly Live with their Children? A New Look," NBER Working Paper #2734, October 1988.

Lane, Terry Saunders, and Feins, Judith D., "Are the Elderly Overhoused? Definitions of Space Utilization and Policy Implications," *The Gerontologist* 25, pp 243-250, 1985.

Little, Roderick, and Rubin, Donald, *Statistical Analysis with Missing Data*, John Wiley and Sons, New York, 1987.

Lawton, M. Powell, "Housing the Elderly," *Research on Aging* 2, pp 309-327, 1980.

"Lifetime Reverse Mortgage Consumer Information for Seniors," Informational Flier, Providential Home Income Plan, July 1989.

Maddala, G.S., *Limited Dependent and Qualitative Variables in Econometrics,* Cambridge University Press, 1983.

Manchester, Joyce, "Reverse Mortgages and their Effects on Consumption," Dartmouth College Working Paper #87-3, 1987.

Manchester, Joyce, and Poterba, James, "Second Mortgages and Household Saving," *Regional Science and Urban Economics* 19, pp 325-346, 1989.

Merrill, Sally, "Home Equity and the Elderly," in *Retirement and Economic Behavior*, (H. Aaron and G. Burtless eds.), Brookings Institution, 1984.

O'Bryant, Shirley, "The Value on Home to Older Persons," *Research on Aging* 4, pp 349-363, 1982.

O'Bryant, Shirley L., and Wolf, Susan M., "Explanations of Housing Satisfaction of Older Homeowners and Renters," *Research on Aging* 5, pp 217- 233, 1983.

A Panel Study of Income Dynamics: Procedures and Tape Codes 1987 Interviewing Year, Institute for Social Research, University of Michigan, 1989.

Panel Study of Income Dynamics User's Guide, Institute for Social Research, University of Michigan, 1973.

Phelan, Christopher, and Rust, John, "U.S. Social Security Policy: A Dynamic Analysis of Incentives and Self-Selection," Unpublished Manuscript, 1991.

Reschovsky, James D., "Residential Immobility of the Elderly: An Empirical Investigation," *Journal of the American Real Estate and Urban Economics Association* 18, pp 160-183, 1990.

Retirement History Longitudinal Survey Documentation, U.S. Social Security Administration, 1986.

Rosenthal, Stuart S., "Housing Tax Policy, Residence Times, and the Cost of Moving," Unpublished Ph.D. Dissertation, University of Wisconsin-Madison, 1986.

Rust, John, "Maximum Likelihood Estimation of Discrete Control Processes," SSRI Working Paper #8511, 1989.

Rust, John, "Behavior of Male Workers at the End of the Life Cycle: An Empirical Analysis of States and Controls," in *The Economics of Aging*, (D. Wise ed.), University of Chicago Press, 1990.

Scholen, Ken, and Chen, Yung-Ping, *Unlocking Home Equity for the Elderly*, Ballinger Publishing, 1980.

Skinner, Jonathan, "A Superior Measure of Consumption from the Panel Study of Income Dynamics," *Economic Letters* 23, pp 213-216, 1987.

Stahl, Konrad, "Housing Patterns and Mobility of the Aged: The United States and West Germany," in *The Economics of Aging*, (D. Wise ed.), University of Chicago Press, 1989.

U.S. Department of Commerce, Bureau of the census, "American Housing Survey for the United States in 1987," 1989.

VanderHart, Peter, "A Binomial Probit Analysis of the Home Equity Decisions of Elderly Homeowners," *Research on Aging* 15, pp 299-323, 1993.

VanderHart, Peter, "An Empirical Analysis of the Housing Decisions of Older Homeowners," *Journal of the American Real Estate and Urban Economics Association* 22, pp 205-233, 1994.

VanderHart, Peter, "A Mathematical Model of the Housing Decisions of Elderly Homeowners," *Journal of Housing for the Elderly* 11, 1994.

VanderHart, Peter, "The Socioeconomic Determinants of the Housing Decisions of Elderly Homeowners," *Journal of Housing for the Elderly* 11, 1994.

Venti, Steven, and Wise, David, "Aging and the Income Value of Housing Wealth," *Journal of Public Economics* 44, pp 371-397, 1991.

Venti, Steven, and Wise, David, "Aging, Moving, and Housing Wealth," in *The Economics of Aging*, (D. Wise ed.). University of Chicago Press, 1989.

Venti, Steven, and Wise, David, "But They Don't Want to Reduce Housing Equity," in *Issues in the Economics of Aging*, (D. Wise ed.), University of Chicago Press, 1990.

Weinrobe, Maurice D., "Home Equity Conversion: Its Practice Today," in *Long-Term Care Financing and Delivery Systems: Exploring Alternatives*, (Conference Proceedings), U.S. Department of Health and Human Services, 1984.

INDEX